Mediterranean Sea

Cape Aemilianos
Vlha Bay
Kalathos
Lindos
MARMARI
Pilona
Lardos
Cape Lardos
Pefkos
Lardos Bay
INKO
M. Ipsenis
Askipion
Kiotari
M. Thari
Gennadion Bay
Gennadion
Cape Istros
Vatioh
STRONGILI
M. Ag. Georgiou
Lahania
Istrios
Profilia
Messanagros
Cape Viglas
Arnitha
Hohlakas
Plimmiri
Apolakkia
M. Skiadi
Aq. Pavlos
Cape Prassonissi
Kattavia
OROS
Prassonissi
Monolithos
FroUrton
Apolakkia Bay
KTENIA ISLAND
STRONGILI ISLAND
Cape Monolithos
KARAVOLAS
Cape Prassonissi

INSIGHT *Pocket* GUIDES

RHODES

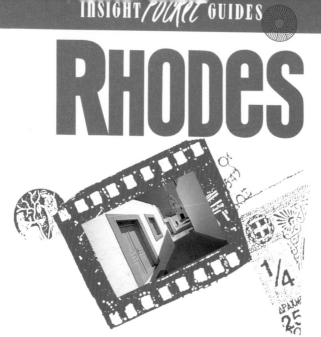

Written and Presented by **Susanne Heidelck**

Susanne Heidelck

INSIGHT
Pocket
GUIDES

Insight Pocket Guide:

RHODES

Directed by
Hans Höfer

Managing Editor
Andrew Eames

Photography by
Presto Press

Design Concept by
V Barl

Design by
Willi Friedrich

© 1993 APA Publications (HK) Ltd

All Rights Reserved

Printed in Singapore by
Höfer Press (Pte) Ltd
Fax: 65-8616438

Distributed in the United States by
Houghton Mifflin Company
2 Park Street
Boston, Massachusetts 02108
ISBN: 0-395-66910-3

Distributed in Canada by
Thomas Allen & Son
390 Steelcase Road East
Markham, Ontario L3R 1G2
ISBN: 0-395-66910-3

Distributed in the UK & Ireland by
GeoCenter International UK Ltd
The Viables Center, Harrow Way
Basingstoke, Hampshire RG22 4BJ
ISBN: 9-62421-513-8

Worldwide distribution enquiries:
Höfer Communications Pte Ltd
38 Joo Koon Road
Singapore 2262
ISBN: 9-62421-513-8

Kalos Irthete!

Welcome! Rhodes, the sunniest and largest island of the Dodecanese, became my home over 15 years ago. To begin with, it wasn't an easy transition. I came here supremely confidant that I had gathered enough in the way of life experiences to get on well with the Rhodians and cope with whatever life on the island might bring. In fact, It was only when I began to love both the island and its people that I felt anything like equal to the task. To this day I frequently feel like an honoured guest who receives more from her hosts than she will ever be able to give in return.

In *Insight Pocket Guide: Rhodes* I have aimed, like authors of other books in the *Pocket Guide* series, to provide an insider's view of Rhodes, directing users not just to the island's highlights but also giving them an indication as to how they might genuinely come in to contact with the land and its people. In particular, this book is intended for the visitor who has no time for false starts and experimentation. To this end, I have devised a series of 10 itineraries, some full-day drives and others half-day jaunts, to suit a variety of tastes. Whether the reader prefers Byzantine monasteries, Crusader monasteries or dune-backed sands, there's bound to be something here for everyone. Each itinerary is accompanied by step-by-step directions and tips on where to eat and drink *en route* (especially *tavernas* where unforgettable views of the Mediterranean come *gratis*) and of course what and where to buy if you want to shop. At the back of the guide you will find all the latest information regarding transport, accommodation and dining.

If it hadn't been for friends such as Elisabeth Aslan, who painstakingly researched the multifaceted history of Rhodes, this book would have been much the poorer. You, and I, can also thank Elisabeth for the richly detailed historical excursion in Rhodes City and Lindos.

Welcome! Kalos Irthete! — Susanne Heidelck

Contents

*Preceding
pages:
twilight over
the port of
Rhodes City*

What to Know

*Following
pages:
fishing
boat bow*

Maps

HISTORY

A History of Foreign Occupation

'In answer to our query about which had been the best of all the occupying powers, up to the present day, the old salt scratched his head and replied that, actually, there had not been any great differences between them. The main thing was to be occupied, spared from independence, which would only bring higher taxes.'

from *The Seasick Whale* by Ephraim Kishon

There is scarcely a more laconic commentary on the history of much-occupied Rhodes than that of the fisherman netted by Ephraim Kishon. Of course, Rhodes has long been and remains subject to foreign occupation, whether by Turkish Janissaries, who held the fortress walls for three centuries, Italian fascists, who propelled the island into World War II or, indeed, by the present-day hordes who roam the narrow alleyways of the Old

Culture

Quarter in revealing shorts and halter tops—the 'uniform' of the latest conquerors. It is indicative of the specifically Rhodian mentality that the locals have adjusted to even this latest, and perhaps most insidious, invasion. From the Ottoman turban to the German helmet, from the leather loincloth to the rattling suit of knightly armour, the inhabitants of this island have, of course, seen everything.

The sun-drenched silhouette of the capital city stands as an impressive testament to its oft changed cast of foreign masters. With its minarets, cupolas and church steeples, its imposing Palace of the Grand Masters and mighty, fortified ramparts, Rhodes City displays its history on its skyline. All this is outshone, however—and shone down upon—by the one to whom this island has always owed its first allegiance: the sun-god, Helios.

Of course, what dry modern science has surmised, the Greeks have known for centuries. It was Helios who brought the island to his father Zeus's attention when it suddenly popped up during the first tertiary period. As a result, he received the island as a gift and, in gratitude, decided to shower Rhodes with sunshine in perpetuity. The consequences of this particular 'occupation' were abundant harvests, wealth and a booming economy.

In antiquity, the island of Rhodes was a bustling trade centre with business connections throughout the entire Mediterranean region. Wine, wheat and oil found international markets as export goods, and great trading houses from Mesopotamia to Egypt maintained agencies in the city of Lindos, which at that time experienced a renaissance of cultural and economic growth. 'Ten Rhodians, ten ships,' was the saying. In other words, whoever lived on Rhodes was automatically considered a wealthy man.

The inhabitants of the island probably owed their wealth as much to the fact that they didn't go around senselessly swinging their swords as they did to the blessings of Helios. Skilled diplomats from the outset, they understood how to maintain what was, of course, a precarious but at any rate largely independent perch between the big power blocs of the day. In times of crisis, they actually allowed themselves to be occupied and then made the best of it. Only if the conditions set by the conquerors seemed exceedingly harsh would they defend themselves tooth and nail. Uncharacteristically, perhaps, they participated in the Trojan War. Apparently, it represented an opportunity to gain prestige.

In 408BC, the three extremely rich municipalities of Kamiros, Ialyssos and Lindos decided to found a city whose location would provide the best possible guarantee against encroachment from the east: Rhodes City. A street grid was designed according to the most modern architectural standards of the time which, in its rectilinear structure, is still visible today. Rhodes City rapidly consolidated its position as capital city and spiritual and economic centre of the island. Cicero, Caesar and Tiberius were students at its famous university; ships from East and West passed through its harbour. An immense number of statues were erected to adorn the new metropolis, the inhabitants of which still numbered some 100,000 at the turn of the millennium—a population density which has never again been matched.

However, from the date of unification with Rome—seen from today's vantage as a great tactical error—the gradual decline of the city began. The island was incorporated as a Roman province of the rising power. Now, Rhodes provided its wine at a ridiculously low price to supply the disdainful and decadent imperial court, and was forced to make large deliveries. Furthermore, earthquakes constantly shook the land and epidemics reduced the population, weakening the island's defences towards the growing danger from the East. In AD515 Rhodes City was completely destroyed by an earthquake. The city built after the cataclysm corresponded in size to the Old Quarter of today. Drawn into the Byzantine Empire, Rhodes had to defend itself repeatedly through the centuries against the advancing charges of the Persians and Saracens. Many of the events of that period are shrouded in darkness, and history alternates with conjecture until the curtain rises again in the year 1082, when two new occupying powers appeared on the busy Mediterranean stage: Venice and Genoa.

It was thanks to the Genoans that Rhodes fell into the hands of the Crusaders. In some fierce horse trading, a Genoan admiral, who was in fact a pirate, bartered away the entire island to the knights, who proceeded to make Rhodes their base for the next two centuries. For the purposes of the holy

wars, and as the last strategic staging point before Constantinople, Rhodes had all sorts of advantages. That what started out as an offensive campaign against the Turks soon degenerated into a war of defence is evidenced by the strengthened fortifications which the knights found it necessary to erect over the years. But, neither cannons nor double walls were finally able to stop the inexorable approach of the Ottomans. Some 70 years after the sack of Constantinople, Rhodes City fell. On 22 December 1522, the Grand Master, Villiers de l'Isle, had to capitulate with the scarcely 200 men remaining to him. Sultan Suleiman I promised him and his people an honourable departure, and the majority of Rhodes' Greek population followed the departing Crusaders into exile. The remaining Rhodians accepted the occupation by the Turks with their usual Mediterranean composure. They looked on as Christian churches were turned into mosques, and acquiesced when tributes were levied to finance the Turkish administration. Since they were

Mediaeval fortifications ring the Old Quarter

View over the roofs of the Old Quarter

forbidden to set foot inside the capital after sunset, they settled outside the walls. On the ground plan of the ancient, spaciously planned city, the present day city, with its tangled network of streets, was overlaid.

By and large, the indigenous population adjusted well to the rule of the crescent. It wasn't until the 19th century that the Turks pulled up short the reigns of power, as all over Greece rebellions rose up against the ruling dynasty. From 1874 on, the Ottomans clamped down on trade, suspended religious freedom, and resorted to violent means in order to quell revolt. However, the course of history could not be altered and, by 1912, the Turks had been deposed by the Italians, and once more the face of the island capital underwent substantial alteration. Huge and pompous neo-classical buildings, which bring to mind the Via Nationali in Rome, sprang up. But though in the years 1922 to 1943, and particularly during the Fascist era, large tracts of land were expropriated, the Italians did much for the opening up and development of the island. Donkey paths were paved and the Palace of the Grand Masters, destroyed in an explosion, was reconstructed. Even today, a marble plaque still hangs there, paying homage to Benito Mussolini. Much was restored and renovated during the Italian occupation, although it could be said that it was not beautified nor, strictly speaking, preserved. Rhodes, conceived of by the Italians as a vacation home for Axis dignitaries, can still look back with pride to many of the achievements of that time.

After the surrender of the Italians to the Allied forces in 1943, Rhodes became the site of many bitter battles which led at last to the final capitulation of the Germans in 1945. Up to the year 1947, the island remained under the command of the British, who restored order to the chaotic administrative apparatus. In 1948, Rhodes became part of Greece.

HISTORY

BC

4000 First human settlements on the island.

2500 Settlement by the Minoans.

1600 Rhodes' Mycenaean Period; settlement by the Achaians, who founded the first cities of Lindos, Kamiros and Ialyssos.

1200 The Trojan War.

1100 Beginning of the Dorian migration. The Dorians divide the island into three regional rulership areas with capitals in Lindos, Kamiros and Ialyssos.

1000–700 Formation of the six-city Dodecanese league, Hexapolis.

650 First Rhodian colonies on Sicily, and in Italy, Spain and France.

490 First Persian War. Rhodes is compelled to fight on the side of the Persians. Victory of the Greeks at Marathon.

480 Second Persian War. Victory of the Greeks in the Battle of Salamis.

478 Rhodes joins Delian League.

408 Founding of the new capital, Rhodes City. Period of cultural and economic ascendancy.

336 Alexander the Great of Macedonia occupies Kos. Rhodes joins him against Persia.

331 Founding of Alexandria, Egypt, which becomes an important trading partner.

323 Alexander's generals divide up the conquered areas, leading to war. Rhodes allies with Egypt for economic reasons.

305 The Macedonian, Demetrios Poliorketes, lays siege to Rhodes for a year without success. The Colossus of Rhodes, a 34m (111ft 6in) tall bronze statue, is erected by the sculptor Chares of Lindos.

304 Rhodes establishes first relations with Rome.

227 Earthquake. The Colossus is demolished.

201 Philip of Macedonia occupies Rhodian possessions in Asia Minor. Rhodes calls on Rome for assistance.

190 Rhodes joins Rome against Hannibal. Victory for Rome.

164 Alliance pact with Rome establishes a more dependent position for the island.

42 Cassius completely destroys the City of Rhodes and the fleet.

AD

50 The apostle Paul lands at Lindos.

395 The Roman Empire breaks up into two parts. Rhodes becomes a province of the Eastern Empire.

1125 Venice conquers Rhodes.

1306 Crusaders acquire the entire island from a Genoan admiral/ pirate. Great works carried out by the Knights of St John of Jerusalem. Establishment of hospitals; fortification of city walls.

1457–1522 Failed Turkish attempts to take over the city.

1522 Six-month siege by Turkey under Suleiman the Magnificent.

1523 1 January. The Knights of St John capitulate. Rhodes remains under Turkish hegemony until 1912. No Greeks allowed inside the capital city after nightfall. New City established by the Greeks beyond the walls.

1912 Rhodes occupied by Italy.

1939 World War II begins.

1943 The German Wehrmacht invades Rhodes.

1945 British troops liberate the island.

1948 Accession of the combined Dodecanese Islands to Greece.

Hippokrates Square in the Old Quarter

Beaches and Watermelons

With a surface area of 1,412km² (545 square miles), Rhodes is the largest of the Dodecanese archipelago which, despite its name (*thótheka* means 12), consists of 14 islands. Only 18km (9.7 nautical miles) from the Turkish coast, Rhodes is the easternmost island in Europe, with the exception of the tiny islet of Kastellorizo. From a strictly geological point of view, the island should be considered part of the Turkish Taurus Massif. However, since 1948, Rhodes has been part of Greece, and Turkish speaking residents represent a small minority of the population, whose second language is Demotic Greek, but whose faith is Islam. In addition to Greek, many elderly and even middle-aged Greeks speak Italian, which was the *lingua franca* during the occupation.

The distance from Cape Koumbourno—located on the 'nose' of the island, northeast of Rhodes City—down to Cape Prassonissi in the extreme southwest is 80km (50 miles). The island has an average width of some 28km (17 miles). The 220km (137 miles) of coastline consist, for the most part, of sand and gravel beaches on the east coast; half beach, half rock in the west.

The tallest mountain peaks are, in the west, the 900m (2,953ft) high Profitis Ilias and the all but barren 1,215m (3986ft) high Atavyros; and in the east, the 825m (2,707ft) Akramitis.

The heavy forestation of Rhodes in comparison to other Greek islands is a result of the relatively high amount of rainfall it receives, mainly between November and April. To date, the island has not yet had problems with its ground water. However, it has become necessary to drill to a depth of 80m (262ft) to tap into the ground water reserves.

The increasing cultivation of watermelons on the island uses up a great portion of the water available to communities, so there are occasional water shortages in the villages, especially after rain-poor winters. However, the northern part of the island, with its large hotel complexes, remains largely unaffected.

There is a stark contrast between the north—overloaded with hotels, restaurants and other businesses—and the south of the island, which is less accessible to tourists and therefore largely orientated towards agriculture. Eighty percent of the commercial activity of the island's population is concentrated on only 10km² (4 square miles) of the island's surface area. Of the remaining area, approximately 17 percent is farmland; 32 percent pasture.

Foreign Exchange and Expensive Cigarettes

The history of Rhodes, which consists of an almost unbroken chain of foreign occupations, has made it easier for the populace to adjust to the modern variation on the old theme: tourism. Tourism has represented the main source of income on the island since the 1960s. Those farsighted enough to invest their money in land at that time were able to buy entire tracts of coast in the northwest of the island for a song. The high, not always well controlled credit policies of the Karamanlis government created, in 1966, the basis for a secure source of foreign exchange, from which the State received up to 25 percent profit. Because of its continually negative balance of trade, the Greek government can by no means eschew this source of income. A monoculture of tourism such as that which exists on Rhodes is, however, more susceptible to the effects of economic recession in the tourists' countries of origin. Ninety percent of the tourism on the island consists of lump sum or package tourism, in which transportation to the island by charter aircraft is included in the price. Individual tourism does not even enter the economic equation, for all practical purposes.

The prices for these package tours have remained relatively stable, since the annual rate of inflation of from 23–25 percent is largely absorbed by the currency exchange rates. However, Greece's neighbour, and antagonist, Turkey, which is still a cheap country in which to travel, has become threatening competition for the entire Greek tourism industry. In order to stop the charter tourists from wandering off to its more reasonably priced neighbour, Greece has ensured that they will lose their return flights if they venture into Turkey for longer than 24 hours.

Thirty years ago, Rhodian farmers were able not only to feed the residents of their own island, but to export produce to the mainland and abroad. Today, fruit, vegetables, fish and meat must be imported in order to fill the needs of the latest invaders. The capacity of the island to absorb more tourists (and it already caters for 11 percent of the tourist load) is being expanded unflaggingly. But the tourist balloon cannot be inflated indefinitely without the danger of its bursting. There are already noticeable signs of a breach, which are expressed not only in the slowing rate of expansion, but also in the declining number of visitors. This leads to empty hotel beds which, due to the sometimes shaky financing of newer hotels, can result in the economic ruin of their owners.

The broad range of EC wares now available even in the villages has been accompanied by price increases which poorer island residents can ill afford. Because of the repeatedly increased tobacco taxes, status symbols such as foreign cigarettes are no longer within the reach of this segment of the population. However, since the island gives the traveller the impression of prosperity, it will be difficult to grasp fully the existential insecurity of the majority of Rhodes' residents.

Saint's Day celebrations in the Old Quarter

Pandora's Box, or Chaos, Greek Style

Some visitors come to Rhodes only to end up feeling that they, personally, have been singled out for a concerted and comprehensive attack by particularly Greek fates and furies: for them, all things great and small can, and will go wrong. It's a foregone conclusion that you, too, if you choose to visit Rhodes, will peek into Pandora's Box and confront chaos, Greek style, in one form or another. It's the look on your face when you encounter all those little demons that you *can* control: smile! The secret in meeting the challenge, and preserving your holiday despite the slings and arrows of Greek fate, is your attitude.

The Traveller as Victim

But there's one variety of traveller who's going to have a hard time coming out on top. This sympathy-inspiring sort has, of

Traditional interior of a Rhodian house

course, already come to the conclusion that nothing works on Rhodes, and he's quite willing to tell you all about it. The luggage conveyor belt at the airport broke down just prior to his arrival (and will probably fail again just prior to his departure). The buses or taxis or both were on strike, too. He couldn't extract any warm water from the tap. His breakfast egg was either too hard or too runny or too this or too that for the nth time. And, he goes on, this list of woes doesn't even take into account the regular power outages and air-spitting water taps. This is, however, not all by far: to his innocent query (which precipitated a public debate) about just when the bus or the ship for his destination was to depart, he received 10 conflicting answers, none of which even clarified the location of the harbour or station. Should you encounter this poor soul, or one of his brethren, be thankful

The Greek *kafeneion*, a man's domain

a similar catalogue of ills hasn't befallen you. But, in case it has, try to ensure you take it all in your stride with the necessary good humour. Fortunately, *you* are precisely the sort of flexible traveller who will be looked upon here as a welcome, long-term guest.

Decibels To the Third Power

It may be that on this island you will find one facet of Rhodian life more unbearable than anything else: noise. Beneath your hotel window locals shout *"Yássou! Ti káneis?"* (Hello! How are you doing?) back and forth at one another as if these greetings constituted a declaration of war. Just next to your breakfast table, a car parks with the engine left running while the driver takes a relaxed ramble somewhere or other. And in the *oúzo* shop, which you find so pleasant otherwise, you are forced to flee as though your life depended on it when the proprietor turns up the volume on his stereo and wailing bouzoukis split your eardrums. Of course, you don't have anything in particular against greetings, cars or ethnic music, but you *do* have something against what seems to you to be the unnatural loudness of it all. You have sensitive ears; for indigenous conditions, far *too* sensitive. Interestingly enough, a Greek ear is in fact nowhere near as sensitive as yours. Therefore, before you froth at the mouth, leading the locals to think of you as being a bit on the eccentric side, try reaching—discreetly—for your ear plugs.

Two-wheeled noise

22

Greek Hospitality

If you should catch a waiter, taxi driver, or shopkeeper in the act of trying to cheat you, you might be easily forgiven for drawing mistaken inferences about the roguishness of the Greek character in general. It would be unfair to conclude that, across the board among these occupational groups, you are dealing with born cheats. Instead, a visitor should realise that he has encountered that unique sporting spirit with which most Greeks are imbued in the cradle. See through this game-of-the-buyer-beware and express your one-upmanship without moral indignation. Your hand will be shaken and in future you will be treated with greater respect: you have proven that you can handle yourself in dealing with them.

As proof of his respect, a Greek will demonstrate a surprising amount of generosity and tolerance, also learned in the cradle. This pervasive generosity to strangers, which you will encounter to a greater degree beyond the pale of the main tourist areas, will take the form of equal parts spontaneous hospitality and trust, which you receive as a sort of credit, as long as you remain an honorary stranger. If you want to prove yourself worthy of this trust, don't misinterpret this 'advance' as a sign of naïve gullibility, but rather as a gift which, sooner or later, merits a gift in return: namely, your own trust. It helps to envisage each intrusion into your usually orderly existence as an opportunity to enter into direct contact with the Rhodian people. In other words, when you get the feeling you have landed in the middle of chaos, Pandora's Box, it's best to mobilise a bit of trust. You will be amazed what wonders can happen.

Rhodes City

Historical Róthos

Rhodes City *(Róthos)* is the most recent urban settlement on the island. In contrast to ancient Lindos, Kamiros and Ialyssos, the date of its construction can be pinpointed. In the year 408BC, the three older communities decided to found a city whose architectural plan would be based on the theories held by the philosopher Hippodamos. The clear and distinctive road system; the admirably located port at the extreme northern tip of the island; the Acropolis, the amphitheatre and the stadium all became within a short time after construction the showplace of a significant culture. Rhodes City rose steadily in stature to become the island capital. In active cultural and economic exchange with Alexandria, the new Egyptian metropolis founded by Alexander the Great, a university came into being here, the library of which overshadowed even the world famous library of Alexandria. Education-hungry students from both the Orient and Occident, among them a large number of Roman emperors, came to study at ancient Rhodes.

However, the strategically desirable location did not bring growth, development and status without responsibility. Over the course of the subsequent turbulent centuries, it was the City of Rhodes which held out against attacks from the East.

The Palace of the Grand Masters

Rhodes City Today

Every year, millions of tourists flood through the narrow alleyways of the Old Quarter to visit the churches, museums and fortress walls, and familiarise themselves with the 2000-year history of the island's capital. The surviving inter-mixture of such divergent cultures, graphically expressed by the city's skyline, combined with an abundance of recreational choices, make a stay here an unforgettable experience. Here, during the day, you can follow in the footsteps of the Knights of St John, admire Mycenaean archaeological finds, and visit modern art galleries. After dark, a plethora of bars await you amid the loud hubbub of the new city. You can charter a boat here, take part in a regatta, attend the theatre, or perhaps simply play a game of *távli* (Greek backgammon) with locals in a quiet *kafeneíon*.

Unfortunately, over the course of the last 30 years, the city has accommodated the demands of package tourists with several thousand hotel beds. In the new city and along both coasts, accommodation now exists in both the upper and intermediate price brackets, attracting visitors who come for recreational diversity. Most of the new hotels maintain tennis courts and swimming pools, and all rooms are air-conditioned. As a result of the package bookings, it is difficult for tourists travelling on their own to find accommodation in high season. Obviously, package tourism has altered the age old Greek world view, and the individual Greek's attitude towards strangers. Instead of Greek hospitality, today in Rhodes City you will encounter the hardened spirit of commerce. To a degree, you must also count on the seasonal unfriendliness of waiters and other service personnel.

In spite of this erosion of personal charm the city has lost little of its magic. If you have a romantic side, you should rent one of the small pensions in the Old Quarter. In this price category, you must not expect luxury. In its place, however, you will find a room with a special view. Just after dawn, when the other tourists are still asleep in their hotel-palaces outside the city walls, your own first glimpse out of the window will include a graceful palm, the cupola of a mosque, a plaza shaded by a huge plane tree or an interior courtyard resplendent with fuschia bougainvillaea and dusky pink and white oleander. Before the shops open on *Othós Sokrátous,* and the façades are obstructed by stridently coloured souvenirs, you may still experience a moment of timeless Rhodes in one of the little plazas hidden away in the Old Quarter.

Pick & Choose

Because touring the interior of Rhodes by bus is not easy, it is recommended that you hire a car or motorbike. Only Tours 1 and 2 to Rhodes City, and Tours 8 and 9 to Lindos are designed for avid hikers. However, all the other tours offer ample opportunity along the way to stop and take a good look around.

A Walk Through the Old Quarter

Half day: breakfast at the Oasis Restaurant on Dorieos Square; Ibrahim Pasha Mosque; Square of Jewish Martyrs; Folk Museum; lunch at the Plaka on Hippokrates Square; Greek coffee in a Turkish kafeneíon; a visit to a Turkish bath; Suleiman Mosque and Turkish Library; Palace of the Grand Masters; Pool and Garden swim; souvláki at the Pandesia Restaurant.

It is astonishing what an attraction tourists exert upon one another. Unerringly, they seem to congregate in the same places at the same times in order, it seems, just to remain together. One of the most obvious examples of this tendency may be observed on **Odos Sokratous (Othós Sokrátous)**, the main thoroughfare of the Old Quarter. As though part of a wave, you proceed up the hill; once at the top you swing off toward the **Palace of the Grand Masters**. While passing by you make a quick raid on the **Suleiman Mosque**, and then blend back into the crowd at the visitors' centre, returning to **Hippokrates Square** via the **Street of the Knights**. Naturally, individualists such as ourselves will put this busy tourist street behind us later on. However, first we can content ourselves by laying waste to an opulent breakfast at the **Oasis Restaurant**, which is situated in one of the most beautiful squares within the walls of the Old Quarter, **Dorieos**.

Sokratous Street in the Old Quarter

Especially in the early morning—English breakfast is served from 9am—it is pleasantly tranquil here, and thanks to a gigantic plane tree, it's also shady the whole day through. You see only the occasional tourist in the square, which has a Turkish mausoleum and peaceful garden as its centrepiece.

In the surrounding alleys you will find small handicraft shops, cobblers, furriers and tailors' shops which have retained their authentic identities: no tourist trap façades here. The **Ibrahim Pasha Mosque** is located in nearby Sofokleous. It was constructed in 1531 and is thus the oldest Moslem house of worship in the city. Its interior, however, is rather plain and lacking in architectural interest, but if the door is open, take a look inside. It is recommended that men wear long trousers if they enter the mosque. The misleading pile of wooden sandals outside the entrance does *not* imply that you should use them: here bare feet are obligatory.

Armed with geographical ESP, you can push on through to the **Plateia Evreon Martiri (Platía Evréon Mártiron)** after breakfast: a map of the city offers precious little help. The alleys are so twisted that you must rely on following your nose or asking for directions. The perplexing hodge-podge of alleys, dead ends, nooks and crannies in the mediaeval city contrasts sharply with the

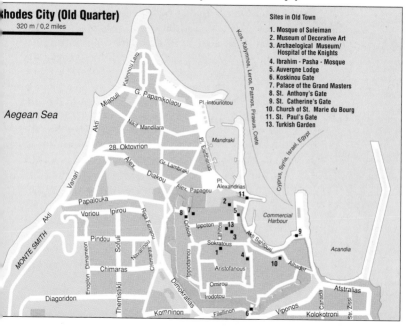

Rhodes City (Old Quarter)
320 m / 0,2 miles

Sites in Old Town

1. Mosque of Suleiman
2. Museum of Decorative Art
3. Archaeological Museum/ Hospital of the Knights
4. Ibrahim - Pasha - Mosque
5. Auvergne Lodge
6. Koskinou Gate
7. Palace of the Grand Masters
8. St. Anthony's Gate
9. St. Catherine's Gate
10. Church of St. Marie du Bourg
11. St. Paul's Gate
13. Turkish Garden

Aegean Sea

Cyprus, Syria, Israel, Egypt

Kos, Kalymnos, Leros, Patmos, Piraeus, Crete

Commercial Harbour

Acandia

logical layout of the new quarter. However, it is still evident on the ground that, in antiquity, both sections of the city formed an integrated whole: **Odos Omirou, Odos Aghiou Fanouriou** and the **Street of the Knights** still run along straight lines within the Old Quarter's walls.

By sheer will, we should now have reached Plateia Evreon by way of **Pythagora Square**. The square, with its little sea horse fountains and shady plane trees, was once the centre of the Jewish Quarter. On Rhodes, Jews made up a significant community, whose position remained unthreatened even during the era of Italian fascism. Tragically, the invasion of the island by the German Wehrmacht initiated a systematic extermination of the congregation's membership, which once numbered 2,000 souls. Only 35 of the primarily Sephardic Jews managed to survive. On the entrance gate of the synagogue, which is hidden on a side street, **Dossiadou**, you will find a plaque which names the numerous victims of the Holocaust. Those who are interested in further exploring the more recent history of the Old Quarter should walk down to the elongated **Plateia Evreon (Square of Jewish Martyrs)** in the direction of **Pindarou**. There you will notice that the majority of the houses are of postwar construction. In this area, the Holocaust extended not only to the people, but also to their homes.

Of course, the walls of

In the Old Quarter

the city hold much more than the memories of just these recent atrocities. The picturesque capital of Rhodes has been coveted by a string of ruthless conquerors for centuries, and what today appears to be the harmonious integration of a diverse variety of architectural styles and cultural elements is really the result of a chain of bloody wars and bitter defeats. Thus, the mosques are really metamorphosed Crusader churches, purged of every representation of the human figure and then topped with minarets. Prior to this most recent transformation, however, the Knights of St John had already 'renovated' Greek Orthodox churches, changing them into Roman Catholic cathedrals. One example is the **Cathedral of Holy Mary** in **Plateia Symi**.

We continue through **Aristotelous Street** to **Hippokrates Square**, a focal point for tourist traffic. Here you can sit very comfortably, for a price, and enjoy a view of the Marine Gate and the former courthouse, which today houses the charming **Museum of Popular Art**. Among the fish restaurants on the plaza, the **Plaka** is especially recommended. Whitebait, red snapper, squid and other Greek specialities are recommended.

The afternoon tourist traffic on **Sokratous Street** should be pretty dense by now, but most of the things for sale here today are tacky odds and ends. Here you will also find, just as in the new city, furriers touting their wares even in high summer, when bikinis would surely draw in more buyers. Despite its overall character, just before the street forks you will find one of the most beautiful cafés (*kafeneía*) in the city, which is managed by a Turkish couple. Here the local men still drink their traditionally prepared Greek coffee and play *távli,* Greek backgammon, a close cousin of its Western counterpart. The distinctive clatter of the tiles is one of the unforgettable sounds of a Mediterranean summer.

After taking a pause for air and caffeine, we plunge back into the crowd and turn left into **Aghiou Fanouriou**, then walk along

Pavement cafés on Hippokrates Square

this narrow alley overhung with supporting arches. By the way, the reduced traffic noise in the Old Quarter is a result of a wise civic ruling. Automobiles are allowed through the fortification walls only in the morning and evening.

Leaving Fanouriou Street, we now come to **Plateia Arionos** where, during appropriate weather, we might choose to take a relaxing bath in a genuine *hamam*—the Turkish **Mustafa Pasha Baths**. The huge dome-roofed main room with its ornamentation and marble floors is used only by men, while auxiliary rooms are reserved for women. Steam baths, masseurs (and masseuses) and an atmosphere of otherworldly calm make a visit to the baths an unusual experience. Located one block further on is an open air theatre where **folk dances** from all over Greece are presented nightly. **Nelly Dimoglou**, the leader of the dance troupe, has spared no pains in seeking out, documenting, and choreographing traditional dances, previously handed down only through 'oral' tradition. (Performances daily (except Saturday) at 9.15pm; for further information, telephone 20157/29085.) Continuing on **Ippodamou**, on which several hostels are located, proceed to the rose-tinted **Suleiman Mosque**, which looms and bristles over Sokratous Street, the newest Moslem house of worship in the city. Every Friday, Turkish Rhodians meet here for prayer services. The

Islamic Library is located right next door, and houses a noteworthy collection of manuscripts.

Now direct your steps towards the **Palace of the Grand Masters**, located on **Plateia Kleoboulou**. A visit to the palace is made more worthwhile if you pick up the informative guide, which you can buy at the entrance.

The Palace, which was inhabited during the Knights' period by the Grand Master and his guards, was badly damaged when the town fell to the Turks in 1522, then destroyed after an ammunition explosion in 1856. It was reconstructed by the Italians (1936) as a summer home for Mussolini and Victor Emmanuel III, neither of whom used it much. Inside, a marble staircase leads up to rooms paved with ancient mosaics from Kos. (You can join a tour around the walls of the Old Quarter every Tuesday and Saturday at 2.45pm, starting at the palace entrance). If your interests are less scholarly, follow the Street of the Knights to one of the exits from the Old Quarter. The shortest route leads through Plateia Symi, with its ancient temple to Aphrodite. In the new city, at the inter-

Idyllic scene in the Old Quarter

section of **Demokratias/Alexis Papagou Streets**, is the so-called **Pool and Garden** where, for about £1.75 ($3.50US), you can lounge around the swimming pool and be plied with food and drink. If you're a non-aquatic species, you can stay in the Old Quarter and enjoy an outstanding *souvláki* at the **Pandesia Restaurant** (Odos Eshylou 49).

A Stroll Through the New City

Half day: breakfast in the New Market; walk via Eleftherias Street to the Mosque of Murad Reis; Turkish Cemetery; Hotel des Roses; a swim and/or a visit to the Aquarium; Amerikis Street towards the city walls; a detour through the park, and Greek coffee on Dimokritas Street.

The **Port of Rhodes** has been, for thousands of years, a reloading point for export goods and remains a duty free zone today. This will be our starting point for a walk through the new city. Before

Mandraki Harbour

setting out on **Odos Eleftherias (Othós Elefthería)**, flanked by neoclassical structures, you may want to have coffee and/or something more substantial in the **Nea Agora (Néa Agorá)**, or New Market, where the new city buys its groceries.

This market-in-a-circle presents a lively scene. Hefty mutton legs turn on spits in little booths. On every corner, *souvláki* and gyro (mystery meat) sandwiches are available. All sorts of meat, fruit and vegetables are displayed for sale by the kilo. Of course, the vulnerable and hungry should steel themselves against the urgent entreaties of the myriad waiters here, and settle where they prefer. They'll find the difference in prices is inconsequential. A fish

View of the Nea Agora (New Market)

market is located in the middle of this bustling circle. This is an elevated, domed building which, with its stylised ornamentation, corresponds closely to the Italian concept of oriental architecture.

In contrast to the new market, which has existed only since the turn of the century, **Odos Eleftherias (Freedom Street)**, down which we now set off, sprang up during a yet later period of Italian building activity. It runs straight as an arrow out to the port and illustrates the fascist era's concern with throwing up monumental buildings, the present-day Bank of Greece and the main Post Office, for example.

On the right, as you proceed, you will see the fortifications which run around **Mandraki Harbour**, the furthest outpost of which—**Saint Nicholas Fort**—was intended to withstand the onslaughts of the Ottoman Turks. According to legend, it was here that the famous **Colossus of Rhodes** was located, though the precise location of the structure, the placing of the great feet, has never been determined. The statue, erected in homage to the sun god, Helios, is alleged to have been some 34m (112ft) tall, but it fell in pieces as the result of an earthquake only 65 years after its completion. For some seven centuries, the bronze wreckage is said

to have lain before the walls of the city, until a Syrian Jew loaded it onto 900 camels and transported it to his home. (More sober scientific estimates have placed the number of camels at 90 at the most.) Nevertheless, the bronze giant was counted among the **Seven Wonders of the World** and has become, along with the **windmills** and the coy **Rhodian deer**, a symbol of the city. By the way, you can see two of the windmills—which are so popular as a postcard motif—from Odos Eleftherias as well.

If you proceed straight ahead, behind the neo-Venetian Prefecture, you will run right into the **Mosque of Murad Reis**. Murad Reis, A Turkish officer serving under Sultan Suleiman the Magnificent, fell in battle on Rhodes in the year 1522. The mosque was erected to honour him. The **cemetery** located behind it seems caught in a time warp—a rather enchanted place with its weather-beaten grave stones beneath eucalyptus, plane and oleander trees. Incidentally, very near here, the British writer Lawrence Durrell lived after the end of World War II. As the British press attaché, he had the thankless task of revamping the newspaper organisation on Rhodes. His book, *Reflections on* *a Marine Venus,* contains a humorous description of these chaotic, postwar years, during which, for a brief time, the native population was subordinate to British officers. (Incidentally, it's a good idea to read any of Durrell's Greek titles while on vacation here, to give you a better feel for the spirit of the place.)

A surprise awaits you when you step into the garden, gone quite wild now, which lies to the west of the Turkish Cemetery. Here stands the luxury hotel, **Des Roses**, constructed by the Italians in 1928. It has stood empty since the 1940s. With its darkened dining rooms, silent casinos and echoing lounges, its interior is off limits to the casual visitor.

Those who have had enough of sightseeing might want to take this opportunity to head for **Elli beach** which begins behind **Plateia Kountinouriou**. On the other hand, those still in search of further stimulation won't want to miss the **Aquarium**, which is located at the most northerly tip of the city. (Open from 9am–9pm.) After the scorching heat of the streets, the Aquarium presents a relaxing alternative with its coolness, its blue-green light and its unreal, underwater atmosphere. By the way, besides the corals, sea horses and scorpions, you'll also encounter such stuffed curiosities here as a seven-legged calf, located on the upper storey.

The way back brings us down **Amerikis Street**, which leads directly into the Old Quarter. A visit to the park which surrounds the better part of the city will be a welcome diversion. There is an attractive café on **Dimokritas Street** under cedar and plane trees, which is sought out primarily by local high school students. Surrounded by their loud discussions here, you can enjoy yet a bit more of the local colour before you plunge back into the touristic tumult of the Old Quarter.

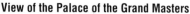

View of the Palace of the Grand Masters

TOUR 3

A Full Day on the West Coast

Excursion from Rhodes City down the west coast road through Theologos, with its ruined Temple of Apollo, to Ancient Kamiros; Kritinia Castle; Kritinia, and its kafeneía; fish dinner in Kamiros Skala (or wine tasting and dinner in Embonas).

This car or motorcycle tour duplicates, for about a third of its route, the excursion outlined in Tour 4: *Through Paradissi to the Valley of the Butterflies.* However, today we will not be turning off for Paradissi but will, instead, continue straight on in the direction of Kamiros. The terrain on the west coast which, from certain points, you can take in in one, vast, panoramic view, is not as wild, steep and fissured as the south of the island. However, the climate is noticeably fresher here than on the east coast.

The first historically significant site, which you will pass after about 20km (12 miles), is the village of **Theologos**, also called Tholos, located about 1km (1,056yds) inland. Here, the remains of an ancient **Temple of Apollo** are found strewn about, the reconstruction of which has been made even more difficult for the archaeologists due to the lush plant growth. Among other artefacts

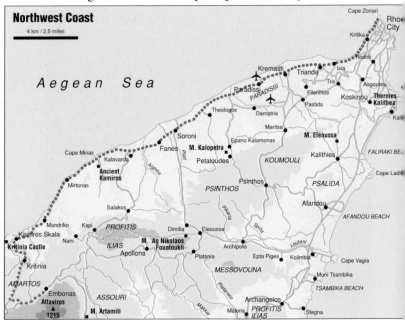

Remains at Kamiros

found on the site was a marble tablet listing the names of priests, eloquent testimony to the former importance of the cult. If you're interested in any and all classical excavation sites, you might stop and take a look. Otherwise, we recommend you drive straight on through to **Ancient Kamiros**, which requires less imagination.

Approximately 3km (2 miles) past Kalavarda an avenue of pines on the left leads to the smallest settlement of the historic Dorian Three City League, Ancient Kamiros. Kamiros was never able to compete with Ialyssos and Lindos, since its relatively unprotected location precluded expansion. Here, however, in contrast to both the other ancient cities, archaeologists have been able to unearth entire residential districts. Fur-thermore, finds from the dig have shown that Kamiros and its fer-tile surrounding lands were set-tled primarily by craftsmen and farmers. The ancient city also produced a significant artist. Ac-cording to scholars, it was Kami-ros' native son, the poet Peisan-dros, who wrote a portion of the *Herakleia,* the epic cycle of the hero Herakles, in the 7th century BC.

The settlement was once dwarfed by an acropolis, the southern portion of which was 120m (394ft) above sea level. Although there is almost nothing left of the former temple city, you shouldn't miss the view from this platform above the sea, which encompasses both Mt

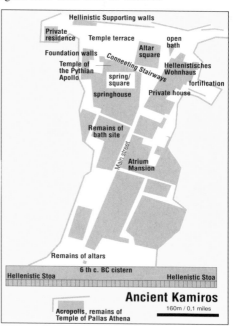

Ancient Kamiros

160m / 0,1 miles

Hellinistic Supporting walls

Private residence
Temple terrace
open bath
Foundation walls
Altar square
Temple of the Pythian Apollo
Conneeting Stairways
Hellenistisches Wohnhaus
spring/ square
fortification
springhouse
Private house

Remains of bath site

Main street

Atrium Mansion

Remains of altars

6 th c. BC cistern
Hellenistic Stoa
Hellenistic Stoa

Acropolis, remains of Temple of Pallas Athena

Profitis Elias and the ancient city. From your bird's eye vantage point, you'll get a good view of the ancient city before going down to tour the site. You can purchase a good guide to Ancient Kamiros, with its cisterns, atrium houses and fountains, at the entrance to the site. (Open Tuesday–Sunday 8am–6pm; closed Monday) After stopping briefly for refreshments at one of the *tavérnes* located below Kamiros on the coast road, you drive on in the direction of Kamiros Skala, which you'll be passing by for the time being. Several kilometres further on, and up, you come to a road sign for **Kritinia Castle**, and turn off to the right on a gravel road, driving straight up to the walls of the castle. This was once the location of the port city of Ancient Kamiros, a site which was heavily fortified by the Crusaders during the 15th century. Today, you can enjoy the impressive, panoramic view—which encompasses both the **village of Kritinia**, several kilometres inland, and the islands of **Karpathos** and **Chalki**—if you squeeze through a hole in the wall surrounding the ruins. Beware the holes in the rubble.

Having made it back to the main road again, a few kilometres further uphill you will come to a fork, and the turn-off for the **village of Kritinia**. A detour off the main road is worth your while now since two *kafeneía* which have preserved their typical village character are located directly in the centre of the town. These **traditional Greek cafés** will be especially interesting to photographers for their rather peculiar colour schemes of pink and turquoise. Stroll through the village to see other interesting traditional structures and architectural elements, all of which make it both charming and picturesque. Kritinia was founded in ancient times by the son of a Cretan king. An oracle had prophesied that the son would kill his father and so the young man departed, and founded the village of Kritinia on Rhodes. He lived there peacefully until his aged father, near death and desirous of seeing his son one last time, sailed over from Crete. Unfortunately, his fleet was thought to be hostile, and the oracle's portent came true.

Now you must choose between two alternatives: wine or fish. From Kritinia, the œnophiles among you will strike a course towards **Embonas** which, with its numerous vintners, promises Greek **wine tasting** fresh from the barrel. (Further information on Embonas, and its culinary and cultural offerings, is detailed in Tour 10.) If fish appeals to your palate more than wine, proceed to **Kamiros Skala**, a small bay where three outstanding restaurants offer a copious selection of fresh fish and shellfish. After an early meal, a dip in the wine-dark Aegean concludes your tour of the historical and gastronomic highlights of the west coast.

Through Paradissi to the Valley of the Butterflies

A half day trip from Rhodes City, via Paradissi, to the Valley of the Butterflies (Petaloúthes); Psinthos; Pastida; Maritsa; the Filerimos Plateau and Monastery; Ialyssos; Tris, and its tavérna.

Set out on this tour as early as possible, because you have a lot to cover in half a day. Naturally, you can lengthen your stay at the suggested stops and extend this tour into a whole day. But whatever you decide, you should take along good hiking shoes and some provisions. One more thing: if you ride, you'll have an opportunity to do so at **Mike's Horses**, a riding stable in the area of Mount Filerimos (Tel: 21387, open from 9am–1pm, and 4–8pm.)

Your route first takes you out of Rhodes City in a westerly direction towards the Paradissi Airport. The great historical significance of this terrain is no longer apparent due to the great number of hotels and commercial buildings that have sprung up here. Villages such as **Kremasti** and **Trianda**, which were lively communities of the **Ialyssos** region several thousand years ago, are today continuously expanding strips of package tour accomodation, their village centres obliterated by development.

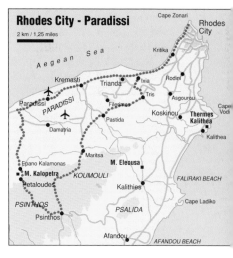

About 3km (2 miles) after Paradissi, turn left into the little road for **Kalamon**. Drive through this village and proceed on. After about 2km (1 mile) you will arrive at the entrance to the **Valley of the Butterflies**. Nowadays, this designation is misleading. The Jersey tiger moths which once gathered here by the thousand, attracted by the scent of oriental amber or sweet gum trees, are no longer to be seen in their former numbers. Part of the blame for this lies in the behaviour of the tourists, who have startled the insects too frequently with their constant hand clapping. Of course, even without the fauna, a hike here is worth your time. The path guides you through a surprisingly green vale lined with unusual trees and punctuated by springs: do not drink from these springs, or even wash fruit in the water. Flowing right through

the middle of the narrow, approximately 2km
(1 mile) long gorge, is a brook easily crossed by means of
attractive wooden bridges. If you want to rest after your hike, you
will find a cosy *tavérna* at the end of the valley.

We continue now on a relatively poor road through **Psinthos**,
Maritsa and **Pastida** in the direction of **Mount Filermos**. Psinthos—
in itself a not-very-attractive town—is historically significant due
to its role in the Italian-Turkish War. The battle waged here on 17
May 1912 marked the end of the Turkish occupation.

If you are willing to make a small detour, you can inspect a one
room Byzantine chapel located just outside Maritsa. Turn off to
the left in the direction of Kalamon, about 300m (328yds) before
the entrance to the village, and continue until you cross a bridge
about 1km (⅝ mile), further on. Five hundred metres (547yds) to
the left stands the late Byzantine, church of **Aghios Nikolaos**, St
Nicholas of the hazelnuts.

A remarkable detail on the otherwise beautiful interior frescoes
are the eyes of the saints, all of which have been stabbed out. The
Turks were not, as is commonly thought, responsible for this dese-
cration. Instead, it stems from mediaeval superstition. At that time
eye disorders were 'treated' by taking mortar from the eyes of holy
frescoes, beating it into a powder and then mixing it into an
infusion drunk by the patient.

From **Maritsa** we proceed straight on to the village centre of
Pastida. Here a street sign points the way to Ialyssos. The asphalt,
however, turns to gravel beyond the village. After a straight
stretch of one or two kilometres, the road forks. The road to the
right leads to the previously mentioned **stables**; the left fork goes
up to the **Filerimos Plateau**, which lies 267m (876ft) above sea
level. If you like to hike, tighten your laces at the first hairpin
turn. Count on a good hour's hike in comfortable temperatures.
Because of the dense forest here, it is pleasantly cool in autumn
and spring. Our route now winds uphill through stands of fragrant
pine and cypress. The lovely views of the Aegean Sea and well
beyond the City of Rhodes are worth the climb.

Filerimos translates as 'Friend of Solitude'. Byzantine era her-
mits, who erected a **monastery** here in the early Middle Ages, gave
this name to the mountain. Once you have achieved the summit,
you will see the remains of an old basilica next to the large

parking area. However, first take some time to inspect the **monastery** grounds, which were restored by the Italians. The reconstructed building, with its arcades, bell tower and interior courtyards full of flowers is very picturesque, even if most experts contend the Italians broke every rule in the renovation. You reach the monastery via an exterior stairway bordered by cypresses.

As is usual on Rhodes, here you will find ruins located beneath other ruins. Thus, the baptistry, which still exists in fragments next to the renovated bell tower, was erected on the site of an ancient temple. Ialyssos, formerly 'Achaia', is in fact supposed to have been settled two millennia before the arrival of the Achaians.

Here on the summit was the location of the religious cult and the **Temple of Athena Poliados and Zeus Polieas**, in which they worshipped, the remains of which lie next to the monastery church.

Those interested a detailed art historian's survey of the Filerimos Plateau can obtain a special guide book from the kiosk by the monastery church. Also available here is a famed **seven-herb liqueur** called koleander, which is brewed by Italian monks and supposed to be beneficial to the digestive system.

Proceed downhill again in the direction of **Trianda**. At the last hairpin curve on the mountain, a sign points towards **Tris**, which you should seek out for your evening meal. This settlement, not even indicated on many maps, boasts an outstanding restaurant featuring refined Greek cuisine, **Qupia**, located directly on the through street.

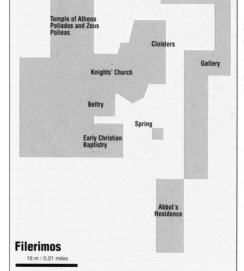

Temple of Athena Poliados and Zeus Polieas

Cloisters

Gallery

Knights' Church

Belfry

Spring

Early Christian Baptistry

Abbot's Residence

Filerimos
16 m / 0,01 miles

IALYSSOS

Ialyssos, in antiquity one of the three administrative regions of the island alongside Lindos and Kamiros, was essentially an agrarian economy. There was no city of Ialyssos, *per se,* but only a loose linkage of communities which lay around the mountain. To be sure, the region, which in pre-Christian times administered the entire northern tip of the island, must have been unusually wealthy, as excavation finds on the slopes of Filerimos have demonstrated. Furthermore, the placement of Ialyssos' fortress—in an easterly direction from the monastery—was most exceptionally desirable from a strategic standpoint. From the peak, the entire northern end of the island can be surveyed. Whoever wished to conquer Rhodes had to attend to Ialyssos, and Mount Filerimos, first.

The Kallithea Hot Springs and Monte Smith

A half day tour from Rhodes City to Thermei Kallithea; Faliraki Beach; Miko Supermarket stop; Rhodes City to the antiquities atop Monte Smith; dinner at the Vlachos Restaurant.

This afternoon excursion south to **Faliraki** takes you out of town through urban landscape dotted with industrial installations, docks, repair shops and intersected by characterless streets. The view remains unaltered beyond the city limits. Building cranes, excavated plots and half-finished hotel bunkers all amply illustrate how every metre of the northeastern coast is being exploited for the purposes of tourism.

After about 9km (6 miles) you will see a sign for the **Hot Springs of Kallithea**. This picturesque bathing establishment was constructed in oriental style by the Italians at the beginning of the century. To be sure, the mineral springs of Kallithea were already known in ancient times. The physician Hippocrates, who was born in 460BC on the island of Kos, extolled their beneficial effects on liver, kidney and rheumatic complaints.

Today the installation, which has not been in service since the end of the war, has a rather surreal aspect with its crumbling façades and dilapidated colonnades. However, with a little imagination, one can resurrect the elegant international coterie in the mosque-like hall, come to 'take the waters'. The park alone, with its palms, pruned hedges, columns, and its continuously changing view of the Aegean, makes a longer expedition worthwhile. After

The Hot Springs at Kallithea

Thermei Kallithea, built by the Italians in the oriental style

viewing the buildings, take a dip in the sea at the little swimming cove located below the springs.

Try to avoid the standard and dull fare served widely in **Faliraki**, which is 4km (2 miles) further south. This village, built solely for tourists, now has some 40,000 beds available. It is a town designed for sport and fitness fans, with a nice sandy beach and good night-life, connected to Rhodes by a regular bus service. From the gigantic water slide to the tennis courts, saunas, surfing and go-kart racing facilities, you will find more than sufficient opportunities to work out in style.

Your return route leads you back via the same road to the edge of Rhodes City. At the **Supermarket Miko**, located to the right just behind the city boundary sign, self-reliant (and self-catering) souls will want to stock up on reasonably priced European Community products, from Irish butter to Italian salami and German coffee. Particularly worth noting are reasonably priced Greek wines and international spirits. A sign at the entrance lists the supermarket's opening hours.

To reach your last stop, the ancient ruins atop **Monte Smith**, turn left behind the small bridge at the cemetery and then drive straight on down Ana Marias Street, on the other side of the main road to Lindos. At the end of this track, turn right into Them. Sofokli Street until you reach Diagoridon, which

branches to the left, leading you directly to the old stadium. However, be attentive. The direction of this one-way street changes frequently, and it is quite probable you will reach your goal via several detours.

If you park your car at the corner of Diagoridon and Them. Sofokli Streets, you can combine your expedition through the ancient City of Rhodes with a half-hour-long hike up a hill called **Monte Smith**. The exciting ascent here is recommended for even those visitors not particularly interested in history. At twilight, the view from the top of the hill, which encompasses even the Turkish coast, is enchanting.

Just as elsewhere on Rhodes, the Italians have tried their hand at restoring the ancient remains on Monte Smith. (The odd and very un-Greek name of the hill originated from a British admiral's use of this site as a lookout.) As a result of their efforts here, the

complete reconstruction of the **stadium**, 200m (219yds) wide and 530m (580yds) long, as well as the small **amphitheatre**, with its marble staircases, provides a relatively vivid picture of the ancient Rhodian lifestyle. On the other hand, it takes a stretch of the imagination to conjure up an image of the glory that was once Rhodes City from the four remaining columns of the **Temple of Apollo** or the wreckage of the Acropolis.

Then, if you are too tired to face the descent on foot, catch the bus No 5 which plies, every 30mins, backwards and forwards between the Temple of Apollo and Mandraki. It will deposit you back where you started at the beginning of this itinerary. You can conclude your excursion with an extraordinary Greek meal at **Vlachos**, an excellent taverna, tucked away on Mikhail Petrides Street, near the Blue Sky Hotel.

Accommodation

In Rhodes City, you will find hotels and pensions in every price range from which to select accommodation. However, hotels in the A and B Luxury Categories are to be found exclusively in the New City. Accommodation rates can vary dramatically between the peak season months of May–September and the low season months of October–April. Deluxe category A hotels cost over US$80–100 per day; category B US$30–80; category C up to US$30.

Rooms in private homes may be rented from 1 July until 30 September.

A: GRAND HOTEL ASTIR PALACE, Akti Miaouli, Tel: 26284.
B: AVRA BEACH, Hotels and Bungalows, Leoforos Trianton, Ixia, Tel: 25284 or 520150.
B: THERMAE, Dimokratias 1, Tel: 24351.
A: RODOS PALACE HOTEL, Trianton Avenue, Ixia, Tel: 25222/26222.
   HOTEL PARADISE, Reni Koskinou, Tel: 29220.
C: The pick of the inexpensive pensions in Rhodes' historic quarter:
   HOTEL PARIS, 88 St Fanouriou Street, Tel: 26356.
   HOTEL ANDREAS, 28D Omirou Street, Tel: 34156.
   HOTEL TEHRAN, 41B Sofokleous, Tel: 27594.
   HOTEL CASTRO, 14 Arionos Street, Tel: 20446.

For more information, contact the Tourist Office (EOT), 5 Archbishop Makarios and Papagaour Streets (Monday–Friday 8am–3pm), or the Rhodes Hotel Association, 1 Karpathos Street, Tel: 27292/26446 who have a complete list of all classes, from Deluxe to category E.

Vehicle Rental

RENT-A-CAR AND BIKES BUTTERFLY, 75 Alexandrou Diakou Street. Tel: (0241) 21330.
INDEPENDENT RENT-A-CAR, Tel: (0241) 24326/35631.

Restaurants

Greek Specialities and Fish Restaurants:
ALEXIS, 18 Socratous, Old Quarter, Tel: 29347/35802.
ARGO TAVERNA, Ippikratous Square 23–24, Tel: 34232.
MANOLIS DINORIS, Museum Square, Tel: 25842.
MARIA'S PLACE, Asgouro, Tel: 62182. (Asgouro is located about 5km [3 miles] outside of Rhodes City on the road to Lindos.)
PANDESIA, Old Quarter, Eshylou 49.
SYMPOSIUM, 3 Archelaou, Old Quarter, Tel: 37509.
TAVERNA HIPPOKRATES, Evridipou Street 10, Tel: 33762.
TOP 13, on Kos Street, in the area of the Hotel des Roses.

Cypriot Cuisine:
MANDRIS, Ialyssos Street 38, Tel: 32574.

Asian Cuisine
SHANGRILA, on the western coastal road between the Hotel Blue Sky and the Astir Palace, Tel: 35914 or 34550.

Italian Cuisine

IL PINO, Paradissi, Tel: 91909.
IL PIZZAGIO, on the corner of Aghios Nikolaou Square, Tel: 25581.
RESTAURANTE ITALIANO, Ippodamou Street 28, Tel: 36931.

French Cuisine

LE MONSIEUR, Kremasti Avenue, Tel: 93777.
CAPTAIN'S, Anthoulas Zervou Street 5, Tel: 26836.
LE GOURMET, across the street from Hotel Miramare, Tel: 26829.
LA ROTISSERIE, Rhodos Palace Hotel, Tel: 25222/26222.

British Cuisine

MOLLY'S, Ion Dragoumi Street.

Nightlife

In the Old Quarter, a deadly quiet descends, usually around midnight.
You will only come upon isolated bars open later than this. By contrast,
in the New City, you can hardly move without walking into a bar: a
veritable riot of establishments exists in this part of town but don't
worry, the list below will help you discover which are the best. In
general, the bars here close at around 2am.

Old Quarter

MANGO BAR, Dorieous Plaza 3, Tel: 85100. (The Mango Bar also rents
out rooms and serves breakfast from 8am.)
CAFÉ CHANTANT, Aristotelous 22, Tel: 32277. Here you can hear live performances of Greek music. Not suitable for the noise-sensitive.

New City

ALTER EGO, Dilmperaki 36, Tel: 32629.
BANANA'S HOUSE, Giva Street, Tel: 36020.
CHRISTOS GARDEN, Riva Street 59. Regular live performances.

STICKY FINGERS, Anthoula Zervou Street 6, Tel: 35744. Live music and reasonable prices at the bar.

LASER DISCO, Koskinou (on the road to Faliraki). The Laser Disco is open until 4am, and has room for 3,000 people.

CASINO: Grand Hotel Astir Palace, Tel: 28109. Admission is free but ties are mandatory for men.

Theatres and Museums

In season (April–October), a Sound and Light show is presented every evening in the area of the Nea Agora. The show is presented in English (Tuesday–Saturday), German (Tuesday–Thursday and Saturday), Swedish and French. Check at the entrance gate for exact starting times. In the Old Quarter, Greek Folk Dances are presented daily (except Saturday) at about 9.15pm in summer on the Plateia Poli. More information is available by phoning 20157 or 29085. Contact the Tourist Information Office for details of repertoire of the Rhodes National Theatre.

Museums

ARCHAEOLOGICAL MUSEUM, in the Hospital of the Knights, located on Plateia Moussiou. The museum holds finds from the Mycenaean Period, and the Marine Venus, a 3rd century BC Aphrodite. Tuesday–Sunday 8.30am–3pm, closed Monday.

BYZANTINE MUSEUM, in the region of Plateia Simi. Collection of icons.

MUSEUM OF POPULAR ART, Plateia Argyrokastrou. Collection of ceramics, costumes and furniture, plus a full scale replica of a Rhodian village room. Tuesday–Sunday 8.30am–3pm, closed Monday.

PALACE OF THE GRAND MASTERS, on Ippotron Street. Displays detail of the city in the Middle Ages as well as ancient finds, plus mosaics, notably the Nine Muses. The palace is a significant structure albeit restored by the Italians. Tuesday–Sunday 8.30am–3pm, closed Monday.

ARCHANGELOS

With its 3,300 residents, the town of **Archangelos (Arkángelos)** is the second largest settlement on the island. The name of the town refers to the Archangel Michael, to whom the main town church is dedicated. Archangelos is experiencing a tourist boom,

and is proud of its **ceramic industry** and **carpet 'factory'**, where you can order a carpet woven according to your own specifications. Traditional, knee-high **boots**—originally worn to afford protection from snakes—are also made to measure by Archangelos' cobblers. (The entire Archangelos village costume, including the suede boots, is unusual, though one rarely sees it today.)

Located above the village are the ruins of a **Crusader fortress**, constructed by Grand Master Orsini in the year 1467 to provide protection against the Turks. **Stegna**, the closest beach, is 3km (2 miles) away and is therefore best reached by car or motorbike.

Archangelos and Environs

A full day tour originating in Archangelos, where you visit the potter Panagiotis; then proceed on to the Seven Springs (Eptá Pigés); and Kolimbia Beach for a swim and dinner; followed by an afternoon hike up to Tsambika Monastery.

It's not necessary to set out on this tour at the crack of dawn, since there are no great distances to cover. Have a big breakfast at one of the numerous break-

Tsambika Beach
4 km / 2,5 miles

fast bars on the main street in **Archangelos** and then take a quick look at the colourful woven rugs flapping in the breeze outside shops surrounding the bus stop. Folded, these carpets will fit into any suitcase and, at approximately £8–10, seem rather reasonably priced souvenirs.

Continue to the centre of the village, where the two main roads meet, and follow the signs by the bridge to **Stegna**. This road through the fields leads you to the top of a hill which has a fine view towards the sea. Here you will turn left and, after roughly 500m (547yds), arrive at the cottage of the **potter Panagiotis**, whose kiln can be spotted just to the right on the edge of the path. As you enter his shady yard, you will probably find him sitting before his potter's wheel. Although he doesn't know you, he will almost certainly greet you as though you were an old friend and offer you an *oúzo*. This you can quietly sip as you examine his assortment of ceramic vessels. (Naturally, Panagiotis accepts commissions.) In addition to the **amphorae**, crafted according to ancient traditions, take a look at his unique wooden bed, intended for alfresco afternoon siestas and positioned at the edge of the cliff above the sea.

After visiting the potter, we follow the road back through the fields and turn right into the main road to Rhodes City, which takes us steeply uphill. From the summit of the mountain you can enjoy a good view of **Tsambika Bay** and, located on the far side, **Tsambika Monastery**, before proceeding down, where we take the left fork in the road in the direction of **Epta Piges/Archipolis**.

Inviting sea and sand: Kolimbia Beach

After 3km (2 miles), take a sharp left turn in the middle of a right-hand curve in order to follow the road up the mountain that leads to the area of the **Seven Springs (Epta Piges)**. The road ends in a parking area adjacent a restaurant nestled in a shady pine forest. A stream flows just below the restaurant, part of the irrigation system installed by the Italians to water the orange grove of **Kolimbia**. It is fed by the same seven springs which gave the place its name. The entrance to a tunnel is located a metre or so from the restaurant and, at the end of the tunnel, the stream ends in a light green pool. Those not afraid to roll up their trousers and wade into the dark will be rewarded by what they find on the other side of the tunnel. However, the faint at heart can reach the place more easily by simply climbing the hill. In addition to the pool, you may want to photograph the colourful peacocks which live on the restaurant grounds.

After a rest in the shade of the pines, proceed back to the crossroads at Kolimbia, where your route continues on the other side of the main road through an arrow-straight avenue of eucalyptus trees in the direction of **Kolimbia Beach**. Here, it's up to you which way to turn when the road forks. In recent years, this whole area has become a prime destination for sun-seeking foreign

tourists, and a series of new hotels and restaurants have sprung up to serve them. On Kolimbia's beautifully situated beach, you will find beach chairs and umbrellas as well as facilities for water sports and boating excursions.

Leaving Kolimbia Beach, we return to the main road, where after about 2km (1 mile) we turn left towards **Tsambika Monastery**. Avid hikers should park their cars beyond the first hairpin turn. Others will want to creep a bit further up the mountain in first gear. The steep little road ends at an interminable flight of steps which lead through a forest on up to the monastery, located on the peak of a cone shaped mountain. Here, a minute, one-room chapel contains a precious 11th-century **icon of the Blessed Virgin**, to whom the monastery is dedicated. Miraculous powers have long been ascribed to this icon. A childless couple found it on the mountain and subsequently the wife, long infertile, conceived. Needless to say, this event inspired many others to make pilgrimages to the monastery, and children born as a result of answered prayer are christened Tsambikos or Tsambika. A phenomenal number of Rhodians do, indeed, bear these names.

The splendid view from the summit, at 300m (984ft), takes in Faliraki to the northeast, Cape Lindos to the southwest and, to the west, the imposing Atavyros Massif.

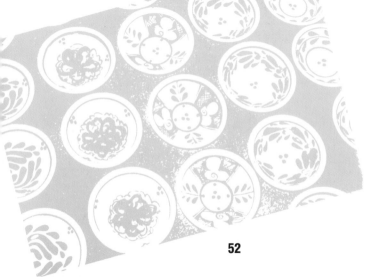

An Afternoon in Malona and Haraki

Afternoon tour from Archangelos, via the old national road, to Malona and Haraki; then, a one-and-a-half hour walk to Feraklos Castle; and a fish dinner at the Argo Restaurant.

Between 3 and 4pm, leave Archangelos wearing good walking shoes, and proceed in a southerly direction following signs for the Old National Road posted at the intersection on the main street.

Haraki's beach promenade and the fortress of Feraklos

After 6km (4 miles) you will reach **Malona,** and the so-called fruit basket of Rhodes. This fertile valley is the site of Rhodes' largest orange grove. The **oranges**, harvested twice a year (end of May and end of October), are delicious, so purchase a kilo of *portokállia* in Malona. They are outstanding as juice oranges. Another gourmet perk in Malona is the village bakery. Here you will find, baked in traditional wood fired ovens, the **best bread** on Rhodes. The fragrant, sour dough loaves may be purchased, hot from the oven, from between 3 and 4pm on weekdays.

For those new to the area the bakery, frequented only by the indigenous population, may be a little hard to find. Malona, and the neighbouring village of **Massari**, are still wholly intact Greek villages which have not succumbed to the tourism rampant at the beach settlement of **Haraki**. Stop just before you reach the little

Fish *tavérna* in Haraki

bridge on the village road, and ask directions to the bakery: *Pou íneh o foúrnos?*

Now double back to the traffic lights at the entrance to the village and on a couple of metres to the right, until you reach the main road for Lindos/Rhodes City. Beyond the intersection, the road leads straight ahead to **Haraki**, whose charm lies in the graceful, Italian promenade which stretches all the way around the port. Here you will find—a rarity on Rhodes—primarily Greek tourists, who have high expectations indeed when it comes to Greek food and drink.

However, before you settle down here for a meal, there's a climb to undertake, the 45-minute ascent to the **fortress of Feraklos**, enthroned on the hill above Haraki. To reach the ruins of this Crusader castle built in the 14th century, go up the steps on the southwest side of the hill. Looking out from the citadel, you will have a view over the coast stretching north from Haraki which is certainly worth all your efforts.

At the end of the beach promenade at Haraki is the fish restaurant, **Argo**, where you can make your own selection from the morning's catch and have it weighed before it's cooked. Red mullet (*barboúnia*), whitebait (*maríthes*) and prawns (*garíthes*) are good ideas. Don't forget that the prices on the menu are per kilo!

Accommodation

HOTEL KATERINA
45 Rooms, restaurant, swimming pool. Around 15mins from the centre, overlooking Archangelos. Tel: (0244) 22169.

HOTEL ANAGROS
26 Rooms. Around 10mins from the centre, panoramic view of Archangelos. Tel: (0244) 22248.

HOTEL ROMANTIC
32 Rooms. Quietly situated about 10mins from the centre. Tel: (0244) 22185.

HOTEL DIMITRA
Tel: (0244) 22668.

PENSION ANNOULA
10 Rooms. Quietly situated about 5mins from the centre.

PENSION NIKOS
11 Rooms. Five minutes from the centre.

PENSION TARALLIS
9 Rooms. Quietly situated about 10mins from the centre.

Restaurants

RESTAURANT SAVVAS
On the main street.

PIZZERIA MILANOS
On the main street.

RESTAURANT KANARIS
Just off the main street.

RESTAURANT TASSOS
Just off the main street.

Vehicle Rental

RENT A CAR ANTONIO
Tel: (0244) 22524/22881.

RENT A CAR TSAMPICA
Tel: (0244) 22145. Fax: 22857.

Tourist Information

TSAMPIKA TRAVEL
Tel: (0244) 22145. Fax: 22857.

Lindos

Ancient Lindos

Along with Kamiros and Ialyssos, Lindos was one of Rhodes' three ancient settlements. This once thriving city, whose golden age began, apparently, with the arrival of the Dorians, sustained itself primarily through seafaring and trade. It prospered due to its favourable, wind sheltered location on the island's east coast.

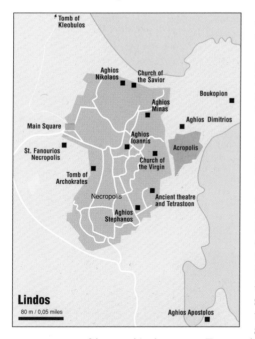

Lindos

80 m / 0,05 miles

As a member of the so-called **League of Six Cities**, it administered the entire southeastern segment of the island. By as early as the 7th century AD, Lindos' population numbered some 16,000. The city cultivated overseas trade relationships and minted its own coins as well as maintaining such colonies as Sicily, Spain and the Balearics. Lindos' law of the seas was accepted as binding for sea travel in general. Under the rule of the 'tyrant' Kleoboulos, one of the seven sages of the ancient world, it developed into a spiritual and cultural centre of international renown. Two marble tablets, found on the Acropolis, record the roster of ancient VIPs: Herakles, Agamemnon and Helen of Troy, the King of Persia and Alexander the Great.

However, with the Persian Wars, its membership in the Delian League and, not least, with the rapid ascendancy of Rhodes City (founded in 408BC), the metropolis declined in significance. Lindos did not regain its position as an important trading port until the invasion of the Venetians in around AD1200.

The Lindian Acropolis

Lindos Today

Nowadays, Lindos is a comparatively small village which, especially during the summer months, threatens to burst at the seams with visitors. Several thousand tourists stream through the narrow alleys of this idyllic village day in and day out in high season. It is considered the island's main attraction, and its historical monuments have been placed under protection as a result. Automobiles are strictly forbidden in Lindos. Still, there are so many British package vacationers here in summer that one gets the impression Lindos is one of the last colonies of the Empire. The streets are lined with countless bars, restaurants and souvenir shops; discos tout an extravagant and licentious nightlife; and surfing and sailing schools as well as yacht clubs ensure more athletic diversions.

That the price of accommodation available in this popular village is relatively high is, of course, to be expected. But be forewarned: non-package tour visitors have little hope of booking space, since most hotel rooms are held exclusively by British travel agencies. You can get information about available accommodation from the Tourist Police, whose office is located in the main square.

TOUR 8

Historical Tour of Lindos

Morning tour: an early breakfast at Alexis; ascent, by foot or donkey, to the Lindian Acropolis, with its ancient temple complex and mediaeval ramparts; a swim, with or without bathing suit, in the Aegean; a stroll by the 'Captains' Houses' of Lindos, followed by a visit to the Panageia Church; followed by lunch at the nearby Panorama Restaurant, overlooking the sea.

In order to elude the hordes who descend on Lindos during high season, you should wake as early as possible—8am, at the latest—and head for the **Acropolis**. By setting out early, you will make the rather strenuous ascent in the cool of the morning, and avoid the long queues at the entrance to the site.

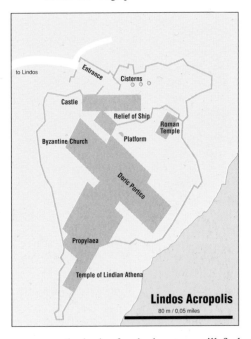

Lindos Acropolis
80 m / 0,05 miles

Today, modern Lindos is a small town, which managed to retain its village-like character through the 1960s only to succumb to the influence of tourism in the 1970s. But from a purely geographical point of view, it is not difficult to find your way around the town. Starting from the central bus stop you simply proceed down the main street. You will find, along the way, directional signs for the Acropolis. You might want to grab a quick breakfast at **Alexis**, located in the first (left) bend in the road. If you prefer to ascend the hill on the back of a donkey, you will find, directly behind the main square, local drivers (and their four-legged transport) ready and willing to help you. Your **'donkey taxi'** will take you around the northern inlet to admire the imposing citadel complex from below.

Pedestrians should make the climb via the stairs, which lead up through the narrow alleys of the village, passing gleaming white façades affording surprising views into picturesque interior court-

58

Lindos' mediaeval ramparts

yards. On the edge of the village, the main street becomes a dirt
path, with steps cut from the stone of the Acropolis itself. Be very
careful here. The uncountable feet that have traversed these stones
have worn down the steps till they are smooth and treacherous. Be
sure to wear shoes with a good grip. If, by chance, you are
interested in **handmade lace**, a local craft, you might want to
pause under the cedar trees en route to the citadel, and take a
look at the tablecloths offered for sale there by Lindian women.

After inspecting these wares, you will find yourself at the
entrance to the **Acropolis**. Purportedly, the site was first occupied
by tribes which immigrated here from Asia Minor. They are
believed to have first worshipped their mother-deity, **Lindia**, a
goddess imported from the East, in a grotto located beneath the
ancient temple site. Lindian myths later merged with the cult of
the goddess **Athena**. The temple erected on the summit in honour
of the Greek warrior-goddess is

Approach to the citadel

supposed to have been in existence at the time of the Achaians and Dorians. Since then,
it has been extensively re-
modelled, expanded and altered to fit the needs of subsequent generations of
inhabitants. What you see
today above modern Lin-
dos are the remains of
buildings which were
reconstructed after a
huge fire in the temple
in 320BC, as well as
a mediaeval castle
which was later in-
tegrated into the
ancient site. As you
enter the site, you

Lush vegetation in the environs of Lindos

can see immediately why the **Grand Masters** built upon the remains of the pre-Christian cult place. The site is a natural, strategic stronghold commanding views of both the island's interior as well as the coast. Of course, in addition to taking in the breathtaking views, you should direct your attention to the Acropolis's interesting architectural elements. Next to the wall of the citadel, you can still find the remains of **ancient cisterns** which supplied water to the residents. To the left, in front of the great exterior stairs, the right-angled steps of which are part of the Italian renovation, you will find an exquisitely preserved ancient relief. It portrays the prow of a ship and, apparently, dates from the 5th century BC.

The magnificence of this site, with its seamless marriage of architectural styles from several epochs, is most clearly evident as you emerge from the defensive walls surrounding the mediaeval command post into the bright, open terrace laid out by the ancients. This was once the location of the **Stoa**, a hall bordered by tall columns, some of which are still standing. Among the niches, Doric columns and remains of mediaeval walls, you will see openings into the ancient system of cisterns before beginning your ascent to the upper terrace of the complex. Here is where the **Propylaea**, a sort of columned forecourt outside the actual **sanctuary to Lindian Athena**, was located. The sacred cult place itself, located at the

Byzantine wall painting in the Panageia Church

very top of the plateau, encompassed an area about 23m (25yds) long and 8m (9yds) wide. Located in its interior was a statue of the goddess, whose official status as patroness of the city of Lindos has been documented as dating from around the 4th century BC. From this high vantage point, you truly have **a goddess's eye view**: to the left, below the Acropolis, you can see the **Bay of Lindos** with its beaches and, to the south, the **Bay of St Paul**, where the apostle is thought to have sought shelter from a storm in AD51.

For the descent from the Acropolis, you should now choose the donkey path, since this stretch presents you with the opportunity of taking a dip in the Aegean Sea: the little **swimming bay of Lindos** is located directly below you. Those eschewing bathing suits should note that several hundred metres further along, the nudists' swimming area begins, though this consists of low rocky cliffs rather than sandy beach.

After a dip, it's back to bustling little Lindos town. The tour coaches, which arrive every half hour, will have off-loaded an enormous number of visitors since you set out this morning. This uninterrupted stream makes the main street resemble a pedestrian mall back home. Despite the throngs, however, you should take a closer look at the façades of the houses. Beyond the walls of natural stone, observe: you may find one of the so-called **'Captains' Houses'**, dating from the 17th century, hidden away behind heavily embellished gates. Because of their rather unassuming and robust exteriors, you will be surprised by the strikingly beautiful interior

Snow white Lindos

courtyards with their arcades and floors of white and black **pebble mosaic**. Equally typical of these little palaces are the balconies suspended over the alleyways, positioned there to guarantee seafarers-at-home an unobstructed view of enemy movements at sea.

To round out your historical tour of Lindos, you will visit the little **Panageia Church**, which is located directly in the centre of the village. This late Byzantine house of worship was erected in the 14th century atop an earlier structure, and was later expanded by Grand Master Pierre d'Aubusson. The interior walls are almost completely painted over with frescoes which were executed in 1779 by an artist named **Gregor of Symi**. Also worthy of note here are the beautifully laid floors of pebble mosaic, which are so typical of the interior courtyards and living areas of the rich Lindians.

For your afternoon meal, we recommend a restaurant located a short distance from Lindos on the road to Kalathos. **Panorama**, 3km (2 miles) out of town, serves shrimp wrapped in bacon on the skewer, and many other delicacies. The restaurant's name is apt, as the site overlooks the entire Vliha Bay and **Lindos Bay Hotel**.

The Tomb of the Tyrant and Evening in Lindos

An afternoon walk to the tomb of Kleoboulos; dinner at the Xenomania Restaurant; a visit to the Qupi bar; and wee hour dancing at the Acropolis disco. Begin in the late afternoon, ideally about two hours before sunset so you will be sitting down to dinner just as the sun begins its slow, summer descent.

From the main square in Lindos, we walk down Kleoboulos Street towards the beach, where we follow the direction sign in the sharp bend to the right to the restaurant **Xenomania**. Our route leads us through a small olive grove to the attractive open air restaurant and bar. Behind the restaurant, the path leads out onto the spit of land which lies directly ahead of you. Continue straight on, towards the windmill before the **Hill of Kleoboulos** with its tomb. Now, we climb, or clamber, uphill and soon find ourselves standing before an impressive monument, originally covered by a half dome roof. According to tradition, this building—which dates from the 1st century BC—is the **Tomb of Kleoboulos**. As 'tyrant', he ruled Lindos for 40 years during the 6th century BC. Consequently, his tomb—if it is his tomb—was erected several centuries after his death. Kleoboulos, considered one of the seven wise men of ancient Greece, has gone down in history not only as a ruler, but also as a poet and philosopher.

From your vantage point on the hill, you have a wonderful view of the Bay of Lindos, the white houses of the village and, towering above, the majestic fortress walls of the Acropolis. Returning back down the hill to **Xenomania**, it is a good idea to select a table at

the edge of the terrace so that during your meal you can enjoy the view over the bay. Here you are, sitting in the middle of Lindos, but far removed from the crowds and din which elsewhere predominate. No dance music blares from the speakers here. Instead, you will hear only classical music and flamenco guitar, and your fellow diners will have nothing in common with the package hordes thronging through the town.

After dinner, a visit to the **Qupi bar** should round out your evening nicely. Stroll at a leisurely pace back to the main square and turn into the alley which leads uphill to the right just behind the donkey 'taxi stand'. Pass the bars called Sokrates and Lindos by Night. About 50 paces further on you will find the Qupi, whose terrace, decorated with Mediterranean plants, is an inviting place to take a seat. Inside the bar, you will find yourself in a restored sea captain's house, decorated with mirrors and Greek amphorae, or Qupis, which gave the bar its name.

Those who are up to it can tour the other countless and, for the most part, tastefully appointed bars of the town. After midnight, a visit to the disco **Acropolis** is recommended to all late night revellers: this lively place is open until 4am.

A Whole Day Adventure Across the Island

From Lindos via Pefkos to Lardos and Laerma; on to Platania and Eleoussa by way of the Founktoukli Monastery; to Profitis Ilias and Embonas, and Taverna Chasapo; up to Kamiros Skala, and the Artemis Restaurant; then back via Siana, Monolithos, Apolakkia, Gennadion and Pilona to Lindos.

From the outset, you should know this is a whirlwind tour, but we will be stopping for breaks. Therefore, by all means bring along your **bathing costume**. Another prerequisite is a **reliable automobile**—with a **full petrol tank**—or a sturdy **dirt bike** variety motorcycle. Your tour will take you right across the island to the west coast, and since we will allow the minimum of time for the return route, you should undertake an additional tour to take in the interesting sites located on the stretch between Siana and Lindos. Either that, or plan an overnight stay in Embonas or Kamiros Skala. Set out as early as possible so that you will not be driving back in darkness.

Leave Lindos via the parking area behind the town, and turn down the narrow road for **Pefkos**. In the morning light, the lunar landscape through which we are driving looks eerie. The isolated new hotels along the road look out of place and lost among the barren, rubble covered slopes. However, once we pass the hill which lies beyond Lindos, and get a glimpse of Pefkos, we leave

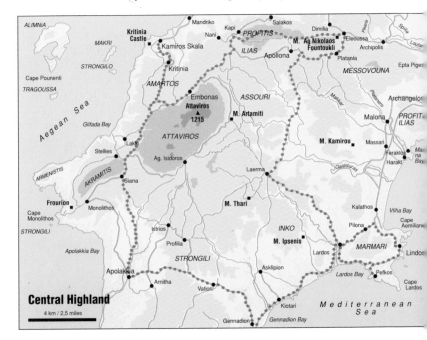

Ruined bridge between Laerma and Apollona

this 'touristic desert' behind us, and find ourselves surrounded by luxuriant Rhodian vegetation. Pefkos, once a rather out-of-the-way settlement in which the donkey drivers of Lindos built their homes, is today a vacation paradise, whose nightlife competes with that of Lindos. In the village centre, we bear right, continuing in the direction of Lardos until we cross over the large coastal road which goes on further south. A few metres past this intersection is the turn-off for the village of **Lardos**. The road leads directly to the centre of the town. A series of cafés here—spruced up for the tourist trade—are good places for your first, or second breakfast of the morning (try Anna's Garden). You can count on prices similar to those in Lindos, however, so be forewarned.

Just behind the village square, a street sign points the way to **Laerma**, and you proceed left and inland. Only a few kilometres out of Lardos, you will see sad evidence of the great island fire which raged here several years ago. Up to now, all efforts at reforestation have met with little success and there is burned forest land as far as the eye can see. This view is a graphic reminder of what can happen if you toss a match or burning cigarette out during a rainless summer.

At the entrance to Laerma, we find ourselves in the geographic centre of the island. The village, nestled in gently rolling hills, has accommodation used primarily by visitors to the **Thari Monastery**, located nearby, in addition to several really original *tavérnes*. (See Tour 13.) Before reaching the centre of the village, we follow the road sign and turn right in the direction of Apollona. After a few metres, the road peters out into a dirt track. To avoid breaking an axle, confine yourself to a speed of 20–30kph (10–20mph). You should not count on being able to get help on this little travelled route. As the landscape becomes ever wilder, you will find few intelligible directional signs. If in doubt, take the widest road.

After about 9km (6 miles) you will notice a watercourse to the right which snakes through eroded stone. The remains of an arch make it possible for you to make out a collapsed bridge here.

Follow the road that leads towards the water. Otherwise, you will end up off to the left in mountains where tree trunks lying across the road will make progress impossible.

In summer, you can drive right through the little stream here without difficulty. However, in all other seasons you should check the depth of the water before proceeding. This is no place to find yourself stranded with a crippled vehicle.

The wildest part of the route is now behind you. Drive on at a somewhat faster pace through thinning forest in the direction of **Apollona**. After about 7km (4 miles) you should turn off on the road that leads right towards **Archipolis**. From here, continue via the village of **Platania** to **Eleoussa**, where you should make a stop in a plaza constructed in the Italian style. The crumbling façades lining one of the long sides of the rectangular 'square' belong to a palm-circled governor's palace dating from the time of the Italian

Italianate plaza in Eleoussa

occupation. In the years since, the Greek military has taken up residence here, and photography is prohibited. Finding the way out of town can be puzzling, unless you consistently follow the signs for **Mt Profitis Ilias (Prophet Elijah)**, at 800m (3625ft) the third highest mountain on Rhodes. Three kilometres (2 miles) further on you will find the Byzantine chapel of **Aghios Nikolaos Founktoukli (Saint Nicholas of Fountoukli)**, dating from the 14th century, and attractive due to its magnificent wall paintings.

Below the road is a square shaded by plane trees where the former monastery-church celebrated saints' days with feasting and dancing. On Easter Monday, the residents of the surrounding countryside gather for a pilgrimage to visit the **icon of the Virgin Mary of Eleoussa**. It is conjectured that on this side of Mt Profitis Ilias many hazelnut bushes once grew, since the Greek word *fountoúkli* means hazelnut. Looking out over the magnificent view from the church, you will scarcely miss the absent bushes.

Our route now continues further uphill through a thickly forested area to Mt Profitis Ilias itself. With each kilometre we put behind us it grows cooler until, on the mountain, we may even see little wisps of fog clinging to the cliffs before we park in the car park in front of the largest building.

No, appearances notwithstanding, this is not some German castle, but instead two impressive hotels, the **Elafos** and **Elfina** (in English, *stag* and *doe*, the island's mascots, which are duplicated on countless T-shirts and figurines). Built in the alpine style by the diligent Italians, in the last few years they have been renovated from the ground up. The hotels now offer A category accommodation, but are open only during high season. After a glance round the game preserve beneath the Elafos Hotel, it is recommended that you drive further on and avoid catching cold. A short distance uphill the road leads, in seemingly endless serpentine curves, to the

Alpine style hotels, Mt Profitis Ilias

other side of the mountain and downhill. At the foot of the mountain, a sign points to the left directing us towards **Embonas**. The village is outstandingly well situated as the starting point for the climbing of 1,215m (3,986ft) high **Mt Ataviros**. Among its much lauded main attractions, moreover, are the '**Greek Evenings**', organised by travel agencies in the capital city. At these events, wine produced in the village is served in enormous quantities. Then, with a bit of encouragement from the Greeks dressed in their traditional costumes, you can dance the irresistible *sirtáki*. In Embonas, too, knitted, woven and lace wares are sold by local women. For those who wish to eat here, the **Taverna Chasapo**, a restaurant-*cum*-butcher shop, is recommended. It is adjacent to the main modern church. While you're here, don't pass up the opportunity to try the **local wine**, or *rakí* (Greek fire water) straight from the barrel. You can have your bottle filled almost anywhere, and save some for the driver later on.

Those who would prefer seafood to meat should hop back into the car and drive on another 12km (7 miles) to **Kamiros Skala** on the west coast. If not too hungry, turn left into **Kritinia**, founded by the Cretans in around 1500BC and today one of the most 'atmospheric' villages on the island.

From Kritinia, as well as from the main road, you can catch a glimpse of the ramparts of a **fortress** on the rugged west coast. Located exactly halfway between Kamiros Skala and Kritinia, it offers impressive views inland and of the west coast.

In Kamiros Skala, you will be amply rewarded for your long trek at the **Artemis Restaurant**, located to the right of the car park area. At any rate, you will be arriving in the little fishing

Restaurant Artemis in Kamiros Skala

bay with its three restaurants well after the midday rush hour, during which the places are flooded with passengers from the tourist buses. Have the waiters show you their wide selection of fresh fish and, if you're in the mood, enquire about the giant prawns and lobsters. While the prawns are imported frozen from Taiwan, you can select live (Rhodian) lobsters from seawater pools. In comparison to other restaurants on the island, the prices in Kamiros Skala are reasonable and may inspire another visit here. Your schedule will allow you to stop here for a leisurely lunch followed by a quick dip in the sea.

Your return route, primarily by way of asphalted roads via **Siana** and **Monolithos** to **Apolakkia**, proceeds, from there, straight across the interior to **Gennadion**, with all sorts of interesting intermediary stops along the way. (See also Tour 11: *A Day-long Tour Across Southern Rhodes*.)

Accommodation

Visitors in the high season should expect to find Lindos booked solid by British and Italian tourists. In August it is almost impossible to get a room. Booking in advance through an agency is recommended.

VILLAGE HOLIDAYS
Tel: (0244) 31486.

LINDOS SUNTOURS
Tel: (0244) 31333.
Rents villas and studios.

To find out about rooms in private homes, ask a local Lindian or stop by the Pallas Travel office, on the main street. Tel: (0244) 31494.

Restaurants

In Lindos, as on Mykonos and Santorini, few people use street names when supplying directions. As the village is small and compact, it isn't difficult to find restaurants and bars. Simply keep asking.

DIMITRI'S RESTAURANT AND BAR
Near the main square. Traditional Greek dishes in outdoor setting overlooking Lindos bay.

LINDOS DELIGHT
Rooftop terrace, Greek specialities.

SPITAKI
In the nearby village of Pefkos. Traditional. Excellent seafood.

XENOMANIA
International cuisine with bar service. From the main square, proceed in the direction of the beach. Turn left at the curve.

HERMES
Refined Greek cuisine; outstanding filet steaks. Below the Alexis Bar.

SYMPOSION
Traditional Greek food. Located right before the Yannis Bar, across from the supermarket.

PANORAMA
Greek cuisine with an international flavour. About 2km (1 mile) outside Lindos in the direction of Kalathos.

Bars

XENOMANIA
For directions to this lively bar see above. Open until about 2am.

STAR BAR
Attractive courtyard bar with upstairs alcove.

JODY'S FLAT
Bar and nightclub, with regular film screenings.

THE LINDIAN HOUSE
In a restored captain's house.

REMEJJOS POOL AND BAR
Stylish place play biliards.

QUPI
Right in front of the post office, this bar takes its name from the Greek word for amphorae or storage vases. Open until 3am.

MED BAR
In a side street to the right of the Yannis Bar. Attractive inner courtyard, video. Open until 1am.

Money Matters

You should exchange foreign currency at one of the two banks in Lindos for the best rate. Do not forget to take your passport, be prepared for long queues, and check the daily exchange rates before changing large sums.

COMMERCIAL BANK
Located in the main town square.

NATIONAL BANK OF GREECE
Located in the area of the bakery.

Banking Hours: Monday–Friday, 9am–2pm, and 5pm–9pm; Saturday, 9am–noon.

PALLAS TRAVEL EXCHANGE OFFICE
Located on the main street. Business
hours: 9am–1pm, and 5pm–9pm.

Post

The Post Office in Lindos is located
near the donkey stand. The service
is reasonable and efficient. Hours:
Monday–Friday, 8am–1pm.

Telephone

The telephone exchange (OTE) is
located by the Alexis Bar on the
left side of the street. Hours: Monday–Friday, 8am–3pm. During
high season, it is also open at week-
ends from 9am–noon. Telegrams
may also be sent from here.

Medical Care

The ambulance service which also
offers first aid is left of the Panageia
Church. Hours: Monday–Saturday,
8am–12:30pm, and 5pm–7pm; Sunday, 10am–noon.

The pharmacy is located next to
the post office. Business Hours:
Monday–Saturday, 9:30am–1:30
pm, and 5:30pm–9:00pm; Sunday,
10am–1pm.

Transportation

Every half hour, public buses travel
between Lindos and Rhodes City.
The central bus station is located
in the main square. It is best to enquire about daily departures/arrivals
and the cost of fares on the spot.

The central taxi stand is also located in the main square. If you
should need a taxi after 7pm, it is
advisable to make arrangements
ahead of time with a driver, as they
are often hard to come by.

Shopping

Business hours: Monday–Saturday,
8am–9pm. Sunday: 9am–1pm. Souvenir shops are also open all day
Sunday. The bakery is open Monday–Saturday from 7am–3pm. It is
closed Sunday.

Note: plastic and travellers' cheques
are accepted by many shops, but
cash payment is more likely to bring
down the price.

Gennadion

This once rather sleepy village was 'discovered' several years ago by northern European travel agencies, which has led to a drastic upswing in tourism in the area and the construction of good pensions and hotels in **Gennadion** itself.

The ample sand and gravel beach features three restaurants in addition to sun umbrellas and beach chairs. The once quaint and quintessentially Greek village shops have given way to modern, self-service stores in which you will now find a selection of German and British beers alongside the rusks and pulses.

Tour 11

Gennadion, and breakfast at the Village Café; Lahania; Messanagros; The Skiadi Monastery and its miraculous icons; a swim en route to Apolakkia; a visit to a Crusader fortress at Monolithos; Siana; Apolakkia; Vation; return to Gennadion.

The best place for a bountiful breakfast is the terrace of the **Village Café**. This popular spot is owned and run by a Greek and his English wife, and they serve practically anything you could ever dream of for breakfast. On the coastal road, we drive roughly 9km (6 miles) right from Gennadion in the direction of Kattavia, until we reach a fork for **Lahania**. Here we turn away from the sea and follow the road until we reach a sign for

the village. An arrow to the left directs us—still before the entrance to the village—to the **Café Platanos**, where the narrow, bumpy road comes to an end. Park the car about 50m (55yds) away from the circular village square, in the middle of which a gigantic and shady plane tree graces the scene. It is noteworthy that this square, in contrast to those of other Greek villages, is not located in the heart of town, but instead at one end. The village church, the Café Platanos, and the two fountains which splash away before you form a picturesque grouping.

It is easy to see why, since the 1970s, a great number of foreigners have settled in Lahania, buying and restoring the dilapidated houses of this village which once boasted a population of 600. In the 17th century, this is rumoured to have been a notorious pirates' lair.

The village population has, in subsequent years, shrunk to about 80 Greek inhabitants, and it seems to have adjusted relatively well as regards the some 50 foreign residents, most of whom hail from Berlin and Munich. Unfortunately, the vintage Greek houses are rented primarily to friends of the owners, so that a traveller stranded in Lahania will have to seek accommodation in one of the rather

The Crusader fortress above Monolithos

scarce private rooms. (Enquire at the Café Platanos or **Chrissie's Coffee Shop** on the upper main street for further information.) The situation should improve shortly with the opening of a new pension. A stroll through the narrow, somewhat tortuous alleys of Lahania is worthwhile if only because they are impassable to wheeled traffic. In addition, above the Platanos, in the **Lahania Gallery**, you can purchase ceramics, jewellery, clothing and leather goods, the value of which lies in their touch of local colour.

Now, we drive back to the upper village street, turning left there, passing the *kafeneía*, and exiting Lahania on the other side. When we have put the serpentine stretch that goes up the mountain behind us, a road sign directs us to the right towards Messanagros. The well cared for road then turns uphill again, through an area of luxuriant vegetation. After about 10km (6 miles), we see the first white houses of this mountain village, where the **chapel** on the outskirts of town is worth a quick visit.

The village of **Messanagros**, with about 450 inhabitants, was already settled in the 5th century BC. The remains of a small temple here date from this time. On this same site, in years following, an early Christian church was erected. Part of its mosaic, in front of the 15th century chapel, is still visible. Unfortunately, the rest of the mosaic lies buried under the village road. If you want to view the **Church of the Dormition of the Virgin**—whose baptismal font and frescoes are worth seeing—you must find Mike, the proprietor of **Mike's Café Bar**, adjacent the entrance to the village, and have him unlock the door to the chapel. However, don't forget to leave several hundred drachmas behind for the upkeep of the church.

At the edge of the village, we turn left in the direction of **Kattavia**, and look for an obscure road sign for **Moni Skiadi** after 1–2km ($\frac{1}{2}$–1 mile). Here we turn off to the right and onto a road which serves mostly four-legged traffic. This track proceeds uphill for only about 1.5km ($\frac{9}{10}$ mile). Then, switchback curves lead downhill—take this section of the route in first gear. About 1km ($\frac{3}{5}$ mile) further, you will see the idyllic **Skiadi Monastery**. You will be greeted at the monastery as if you were long lost friends. The couple who care for the grounds are always ready to receive visitors, including those who wish to spend the night there.

The well kept grounds, with their buildings dating from the 18th and 19th centuries, sprang up around a Church of the Holy Cross which was erected in the 13th century, then enlarged with a broad nave in the 19th century. In the interiors of these buildings are found the legendary **icons of The Panageia (The Blessed Virgin)** from Skiadi, which are said to weep tears of blood on their 'namedays'. Over the Easter period, they are carried from village to village until, finally, they come to rest for a whole month on the island of Chalki. Also, on 8 September, when the annual church festival of Skiadi takes place, the Panageia icons are reverently worshiped by people streaming in from the length and breadth of the surrounding region. Afterwards, there is a celebration with live music and dancing, which lasts all night long.

Before setting off on the next leg of your trip, to the sea and Apolakkia, enjoy the wonderful view of the **Koukouliari Mountains** and the west coast while sipping Greek coffee at the monastery. Please be sure to leave the devout caretakers a generous donation.

When you reach the connecting road between Kattavia and Apolakkia, which is to date only partially paved, turn right and park on one of the paths branching off to the left. Stroll down to the sea for a refreshing swim. But keep in mind that powerful summer breakers produce undercurrents in various places on the west coast. Do not venture too far out to sea unless you are a really outstanding swimmer.

After your swim, it's just a few kilometres to **Apolakkia**, where you should stop in the central *plateía* and have a snack. All four of the *tavérnes* surrounding the square are worth recommending and have kept their prices reasonable. (If you haven't any idea what to order, try one of the excellent cheese omelettes.)

From the *plateía,* follow the road signs to **Monolithos**, a mountain village some 11km (7 miles) further on through luxuriant green forest. We cut through this village which has, unfortunately, been discovered by tourism, on its upper main street, and follow the sign for the **Frourion** (fortress). Just 1km (³⁄₅ mile) past the village, you can glimpse the Crusader stronghold enthroned on a 230m (755ft) high chalk cliff—the only attraction of Monolithos.

The breathtaking view makes the short hike worthwhile. It begins in a bend in the road beneath the observation point. Once you have arrived you will find, surrounded by the remains of fortress walls, a little white chapel under wind gnarled pines, the arches of a chapel of older date, and the foundations of a square building. It doesn't require much imagination to see that the

knights could here keep track of all shipping moving towards Crete and North Africa.

To reach **Siana**, you must now cut through Monolithos again, retracing your tracks, then drive straight on for about 7km (4 miles). Park your car just behind the village church next to the **Café-Bar Manos**, and take a look into this typical village *kafeneíon,* with its enchanting view over the mountainous surrounding landscape. Here, you are at the source of *soúma* and honey, which the friendly proprietors sell to travellers. The *soúma,* strongest in the autumn, is a liquor made from grapes, distilled only in this village. Mystical qualities are ascribed to it. Try out a glass and see for yourself.

You are now ready to start out on the return route, which first leads back to Monolithos and Apolakkia. On the *plateía,* however, do not turn right towards Kattavia. Instead, go left towards Gennadion. Several kilometres further, turn to the right to Arnitha. But you must, in fact, bear left, though the road signs do not indicate this. Proceed uphill and, once you have put the summit of the mountain behind you, you are nearing the village of **Vation**, only 7km (4 miles) from Gennadion.

Vation is worth a little side trip. Allow yourself an *oúzo* on the plane tree shaded village square in the company of the primarily elderly villagers before driving back to Gennadion. Here you can still experience something of the friendly composure and quiet of untouched rural Greece.

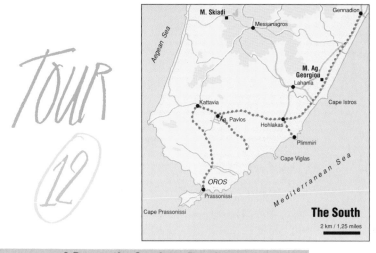

A Day on the Southern Beaches

From Gennadion; sun and swimming at Hawaii Beach; Cape Prassonissi; Greek coffee at Kattavia; a seafood meal at Plimmiri. This tour is dedicated primarily to the pleasures of swimming, sunning and relaxing under the southern sun.

Sleep your fill and then start out from Gennadion in the direction of Kattavia after a generous breakfast at **Klimis**, on the beach. After roughly 16km (10 miles), having passed by the point where the road branches off towards Plimmiri, you will notice two avenues on the left which were laid out by the Italians. This was once the settlement of **Aghios Pavlos**, the location of a prison dating from the Italian occupation, which is used today as a pig farm. We turn into the first of the two avenues and drive along the country road towards the sea, till the way ends in sparsely vegetated sand dunes. Behind the dunes, you will see a broad, sandy beach, usually deserted. If you start out from here and hike to the right along the beach (*not* barefoot), after about 10mins you will arrive at the end of the elongated bay, and a spot protected from the wind and shaded by cliffs. Stay here for a wonderful hour or two of swimming, sun and seashell gathering.

The southern tip of Rhodes: Prassonissi

Continuing on from Aghios Pavlos, we follow the main road for about 3km (2 miles) in the direction of **Kattavia**, where we keep to the left at the fork just outside the village. Some 100m (109yds) further you will see a road sign for **Prassonissi**, which leads to the left on a 7km (4 mile) long gravel road to the southern tip of the island. Here, west and east coasts meet. The strong wind which prevails here most of the time attracts surfers who graduate from intermediate to advanced by riding these large breakers. You will also find here two relatively new *tavérnes* serving fresh fish at the narrow isthmus to the little peninsula which stretches out beyond Prassonissi. For the time being, you should deny yourself another ample meal and, instead, depending on the weather (in winter the sandy connecting spit is flooded), take a half-hour stroll to the **lighthouse** on the other side of the peninsula. However, do not at-

Fishing boat in Plimmiri bay

tempt to cover this distance by car since it's quite possible you'll get stuck in the sand. A motorcycle is much more suitable, if your feet are really that tired.

Back at the fork in the main road, you can either turn off to the right towards Plimmiri, or drive straight ahead, on the other side of the main road, and pay a brief visit to the village of **Kattavia**. After 200m (219yds), you will find yourself in the central *plateía*, which is surrounded by several *kafeneía*. At the **Café Tofos**, you can take a seat in the shade of an expansive tree and study the

Church in Plimmiri

languid village life of the residents who have, for the most part, been spared from the ravages of tourism. The only variation in the texture of village life is brought about by the military who are stationed in the area.

Since you are probably rather hungry by now, drive 8km (5 miles) back down the main road to the fork for **Plimmiri**, which is at the end of a 1.5km (1 mile) long side street. The outstanding Fish Restaurant of **Yannis Galantomos** and the romantic view over the little fishing bay, on which a longer swimming beach is located, is likely to extend the time of your stay in Plimmiri. If you should happen to walk to the hills behind the restaurant, on the heights you will discover a series of residential ruins which date from the German occupation. To the right of these, the ancient city of **Kyrbe** is said to have stood. However, it fell victim to a flood (Greek: *plimmiri*), hence the name of the village below. A later village believed to have existed here was called **Ixia**.

The church which is located just behind the restaurant was itself erected atop the foundation walls of a much earlier Christian basilica, whose columns and marble work have been incorporated into the present building. In the front yard of the church there is a pond which was once the site of a spring said to have miraculous powers.

A Motorcycle Tour of the Southeast Coast

A half day tour from Gennadion; to Kiotari; Asklipion; the Thari Monastery; Laerma; and Lardos.

We will be leaving the village of **Gennadion** on the coast road heading north. Pass a petrol station and continue on to the intersection for **Asklipion** (left) and **Kiotari** (right). Bearing right, you will find another beach equally as beautiful as the one at Haraki, which calls for a break. Pull off the road and take a swim. Although many well situated restaurants can be found here, **Stefan**

Laerma / Asklipion / Lardos

4 km / 2,5 miles

(on the left) serves the best fish. Ask to see the day's catch, and remember that Rhodes is famous for its red mullet, swordfish and lobster. Stay on the coast road for Asklipion. You will pass a chapel and, adjacent, the home of the local priest, but continue on into the village centre, where the **oldest extant church** on the island stands. Ask at the *kafeneíon* for the key, and you're sure to find assistance. The 17th century frescoes in this church make the effort well worthwhile.

You will be able to discern the ruins of **Iannis Castle** on a hilly area near the village centre. This represents one of the most southerly points of fortification on the south coast.

Leave the village via one of the upper streets, and head northwest for about 7km (4 miles) via the road for **Laerma** and **Moni Thari** (**Thari Monastery**). This will take you diagonally through a forest. Two kilometres (about 1 mile) before you reach Laerma, you will see one of the island's most precious treasures. Legend has it that a Byzantine princess, afflicted with a fatal illness, had this monastery built so that she might retreat to the wilderness and there die in peace. The monastery was duly built, and the princess miraculously recovered. The picturesque monastery buildings were most probably erected between the 9th and 13th centuries, although the foundations date from before the Christian era.

After visiting the church and abandoned monks' cells at the Thari Monastery, do take this opportunity to set out for a lengthy jaunt in the surrounding countryside. Along your way, you will easily see why the area was selected as the venue for a huge annual festival which is held every June. Thousands of people from all over Rhodes and elsewhere gather here to feast and dance the night away. (Wherever you are in Greece, it is especially worthwhile to find out what festivals, *yortés*, or Saints' days will fall within your stay. Attending these events is the best way to get to know the Greeks as well as enjoy yourself.)

From the monastery, proceed in the direction of **Laerma**, where several *kafeneía* will tempt you in for a refreshing pause. Try a Greek 'spoon sweet', *glikó koutalioú*, with your coffee. Continue on towards **Lardos**. Ask for directions to the workshop of **Lynn Fischer**, whose **ceramics** represent a departure from most ware to be found on Rhodes (see picture on page 85).

Tourist Information

PALLAS TRAVEL
Tel: (0244) 43340. Hours: Monday–Saturday, 9am–1pm; 5pm–8:30pm.

Accommodation

TINA'S APARTMENTS
For information, contact Pallas Travel.
BETTY STUDIOS AND APARTMENTS
In the centre of town.
IRENE'S PENSION
In the centre of town.
DENNIS BEACH STUDIOS
Outside the town centre on the beach; contact Pallas travel.
KIOTARI VIEW
Tel: (0244) 43349).

Restaurants

KLIMIS
On the beach, with an attractive terrace, and reasonable prices.
ANTONIS
On the beach, with a beautiful terrace, and outstanding food. Tel: (0244) 43300.
ST GEORGE
About 1km (⅝ mile) past Gennadion on the coastal road towards Kattavia. Tel: (0244) 43267.

ROBERT'S
In the main street, British ambience.
EL GRECO
Between OTE (the telephone exchange) and the Post Office.
THE THREE BROTHERS
On the coast road.

Cafés & Bars

CAFÉ MEMORIES
Next to the supermarket.
VILLAGE CAFÉ
On the main street.

Vehicle Rental

KOALA RENT-A-CAR
Right at the entrance to the village. Tel: (0244) 43304.
TEO RENT-A-CAR
Lahania, reasonable rates. Tel: (0244) 43390.
EXPLORER RENT-A-MOTO
Tel: (0244) 43256.

Medical Station

On the coastal road at the entrance to the village.

International Press

THE THREE MILLS
In the village centre. Tel: (0244) 43033.

Dining Experiences

Traditional Greek fare, as prepared in private Greek homes, is varied and subtle, in contrast to the food commonly available in *tavérnes* catering for the general public, and tourists in particular. In *tavérnes* frequented by the Greeks themselves, you will find a limited number of dishes, indifferently prepared as a rule. (Sensible Greeks eat at home, where labour intensive specialities are lovingly prepared.) Among the starters you'll find on a *tavérna* menu are **tsatzíki**, a yoghurt, garlic and cucumber dip, containing fresh dill if you're lucky; **dolmáthes**, grape leaves filled with seasoned rice and/or meat; **táramasaláta**, a dip made of fish roe, bread and/or potato and oil; and the irresistible **horiátiki saláta** (literally, village salad), which in winter consists of finely chopped white cabbage and, in summer, of tomato, cucumber, onion, *féta* cheese and olives.

Main dishes on *tavérna* menus include pork cutlets, roasted lamb, **souvláki** (grilled chunks of pork or lamb), **stifádo** (a spicy stew, beef or rabbit), **moussaká** (a casserole of eggplant, potato, minced meat and bechemel), **pastítsio** (Greek lasagna) and **yemistés/á**, tomatoes, peppers, zucchinis or eggplants stuffed with rice and minced meat. Side dishes, such as **patátes tiganités** (chips) must be ordered separately.

Fish appears on the menus in two price categories generally quoted per kilogram, not per portion. The fish considered best by Greeks and, at any rate, the most expensive, are **barboúnia** (red mullet) and swordfish. Cheaper, though sometimes chewy, are **kalamária** (fried squid) and grilled octopus.

In the tourist centres, a sort of international cuisine has been introduced, in which pizza and pepper steak are star players. In Rhodes City, fast food restaurants have sprouted up, crowding out the traditional *gyro* and *souvláki* stands. The use of microwave ovens has also become such an epidemic that dishes which were traditionally served at room temperature now burn your tongue.

Tipping customs are as follows. In addition to the service charge already included in the price of your meal, a 5–10 percent tip should be given. Don't forget to leave something for the assistant waiter who clears the dishes and earns very little for his pains.

Beverages

On any occasion, as an apéritif, after meals, as well as in between, **oúzo**, a liqueur flavoured with anise, is appropriate. In the countryside it is drunk undiluted, taken in sips alternating with sips of cold water. In the city, it is also served with ice or mixed with cold water. A little glass of *oúzo* consumed at the appropriate time settles the stomach and quiets the mind. The national drink is expressive of the Greek way of life. In the *kafeneía,* it is usually served by the glass or in a *karafáki,* or small carafe. Unfortunately, the custom of serving *mezéthes,* morsels of cucumber and cheese, olives or nuts, along with the traditional *oúzo,* is dying out.

Greek coffee, which faces strong competition from the ubiquitous Nescafé, is consumed either *glikó* (sweet), *métrio* (medium) or *skéto* (without sugar). Sugar is not served on the side. Instead, it is boiled along with the coffee. The grounds remain at the bottom of the cup as you drink, and should stay there.

Wine is normally dry. However, all varieties designated 'demi-sec' are sweet. The wines offered in the majority of restaurants come from the large bottling firms of Caïr and Emery, which more or less control the island's wine production. Caïr distributes the Ilios (white) and Chevalier (red) labels as well as the expensive white, red and rosé Moulin. Emery wines, whose prices are almost identical to those of the competition, are to be had in white and rosé. Beyond Caïr and Emery, some table wines worth recommending are the Calliga, Boutari, Nemea and Apelia labels. **Retsína**, or resin flavoured wine, is not for everyone. Less than half the price of non-resinated on most menus, it's an acquired taste. Kourtaki is a good one to sample.

Beer is well on the way to pushing aside wine on the Greek table. Among the beers produced under license, such as Henninger, Löwenbräu, Amstel and Heineken, the last leads the pack. Greeks, it should be said, generally prefer an icy Amstel.

Shopping

Rhodes has stocked its supermarket shelves to keep up with the requirements of visitors from the north. In all the larger stores you will find the products you use at home in England, America and Australia. This is especially good news for those self-reliant or self-catering souls who refuse to forego their continental or English breakfast, complete with marmalade, bacon, eggs and/or muesli. Furthermore, there are off licenses everywhere, though their prices have skyrocketed in recent years. Still, purchasing spirits on Rhodes is worth your while, since alcoholic beverages are still around 20 to 30 percent cheaper than in much of the rest of Europe.

Tobacco products are a similar bargain. A carton of cigarettes manufactured under Greek license (Marlboro, Camel etc) costs about 40 percent less on Rhodes than in England, for example. Even more reasonably priced are domestic cigarettes such as Assos, and the popular Karellias.

Souvenirs In Rhodes City you will find **jewellery** shops on every corner where distinctive 'Greek gold' designs sell for comparatively reasonable prices. Of course, the art of gold working has a long tradition on Rhodes, though most of the jewellery sold on the island today is produced in Italy.

The Athens based jeweller **Ilias Lalaounis** maintains a shop on the former Auberge de l'Auvergne, where flawless copies of ancient designs and collections featuring Byzantine elements, rock crystal or pavé diamonds may tempt you.

In the city, **leathers and furs** are also offered for sale. This may seem rather peculiar considering the often sweltering heat. One of the best shops is **Dano Niko**, 92 Socratour Street, which also stocks vibrant kilims made in the village of Embonas.

Ceramics, embroidery and woven carpets are also traditional Rhodian products, but the quality is variable.

Hand painted ceramics can be found at **Phidias**, on Panetou Street. The motifs on this ware are based on ancient patterns though more modern designs are also available. Equally worthy of mention are **O Myrina**, on Griva Street, where you can also buy

ceramic figurines, and the **Greek Gallery**, 74 Socratous Street. Rhodian ceramics it should be noted, are famous throughout Greece. Traditional designs are outlined in black on a white or cream background, then hand painted in bold colours. Lamps and huge platters will add stunning accents to monochrome rooms back home. Located in the area of Archangelos (see Tour 7: *An Afternoon in Malona and Haraki*) is the **pottery workshop** of **Panagiotis**, who produces amphorae in the old style, pots and bowls, and other ware. His ceramics are unpainted for the most part, but the simple, pleasing shapes of his everyday articles are decoration enough. Right on the main road as you enter the village of Archangelos is the **Neofitou Ceramic Manufactory**, where you can obtain fine copies of ancient ceramics.

You can purchase **handmade lace** most reasonably in Lindos, where this art has long been practised. (See Tour 8: *Historical Tour of Lindos*.) In Archangelos and Afantou, you can buy beautifully made woven **carpets and runners** at remarkably low prices, as well as handmade traditional **boots**. In Siana, a small mountain village on the west coast (See Tour 12: *The Southern Beaches*), you can obtain superior quality **honey** and **soúma**, a homemade grape spirit which comes close in taste to Italian *grappa*. You can buy **wine** in bulk at Embonas. Also located here is the largest wine company in the region, Emery.

Travel To and From Rhodes

The most comfortable way to reach Rhodes is by air. Although you can never be sure that the airport bank will be open upon your arrival, you can exchange money at any time, at a reasonable rate of exchange, at the Olympic counter. It is here, too, that tickets for the bus transfer to Rhodes City are sold.

The Olympic Airways Bus, which runs to complement Olympic Airways arrivals/departures is the most comfortable and economical way to get to the new city (16km/26 miles away). It goes directly to the Olympic Airways City Office, which is centrally located.

In addition, there is a regularly scheduled public bus for Rhodes City which stops outside the airport.

A taxi to the centre of Rhodes City costs about £3.50 ($7US). If another passenger turns up going the same way as you, do not be surprised when the taxi driver charges you both the full fare. In Greece this is 'legal', if not the letter of the law.

Those arriving by ship don't have far to go, especially if they are bound for the Old Quarter, whose walls end at the port. A bus or taxi from the ship is hardly worth the fare.

Customs and Duties

All articles for personal use may be brought into Greece duty free. If there is any doubt as to the strictly personal use of an item—a typewriter, for example, a television or video recorder— you may have it entered in your passport so that when you depart it can be ascertained that you are 'exporting' the item with you.

For goods from the duty free shop, there are the following free limits: 200 cigarettes, 1 litre of spirits and 2 litres of wine.

For goods not purchased in the duty free shop, the free limits are somewhat higher: 3,000 cigarettes, 1.5 litres of spirits and 5 litres of wine.

Changes in Booking

Changes in booking for charter flight ticket holders can be taken care of in most cases without difficulty by the individual carriers' agents in Rhodes City. A prerequisite for changing your ticket is the availability of a corresponding seat on another aircraft. Naturally, you must pay the telex costs and re-booking fees, which vary from case to case.

If your re-booking efforts in cases of emergency or illness prove fruitless, you can try to re-book your flight at your carrier's airport check-in counter. If there is a seat available on one of your carrier's aircraft (due to a no-show, perhaps), then the airport manager will probably give you permission to leave without changing your ticket, upon the presentation of a legal affidavit stating your problem.

MONEY MATTERS

Banks
Hours: Monday–Friday 8am–2pm. Some exchange counters, and all private exchange bureaux are also open in the evening.

Currency
The Greek monetary unit is the drachma. It is divided into 100 lepta, which no longer exist as coins. There are 1, 2, 5, 10, 20, and 50-drachma coins. The paper bills come in 100, 5000, 1,000 and 5,000-drachma denominations.

CLIMATE & GEOGRAPHY

Time Zones
Greek time is two hours ahead of Greenwich Mean Time.

Air Temperatures
On Rhodes, summer does not arrive until May, when an average of 25°C (77°F) prevails. June, at almost 30°C (86°F), is considerably hotter, but August, when the mercury reaches a high of around 33°C (91°F), is blistering. Visitors should bring sunblock, and wear hats and long sleeves to avoid dangerous burns even in spring.

In September, June temperatures return, and in October those of May. January and February, at around 16°C (61°F), are easily the coldest months of the year. Statistics for the island record peak temperatures of over 40°C (104°F) and lows of nearly freezing.

Sea Temperatures
You will rarely see a Greek in the sea before the beginning of June, in other words not until the water temperature reaches about 21°C (70°F). Tourists arriving from cooler countries are not so sensitive: they jump into the water in May, when the water temperature is 19°C (66°F). By August the water has warmed to about 25°C (77°F), so a dip in the sea is no longer

bracing. In October, the temperature sinks again to about 22°C (72°F) and reaches the lowest levels of the year in February and March: 16°C (61°F).

Wind
When the weather is hot, from May till September, the wind known as the *meltémi* blows in from the north to cool brows and tempers. It blows primarily between morning and sunset, and it can reach a wind strength of 5 or 6 on the Beaufort Scale. If it climbs to 7 or 8, it can blow on through the night. Occasionally, during the day, it manages to spirit a coffee cup right off a table but, on the whole, visitors

are grateful for the cooling effects of this summer breeze.

In antiquity, Aeolos, the son of the sea god Poseidon, was considered the creator of the *meltémi*. Today, it is known that strong air pressure gradients between the western and eastern Mediterranean produce these vigorous air movements.

Rainfall

From the beginning of June until the end of August you can be sure that not one drop of rain will fall on Rhodes, even if you occasionally wish one would. April and May average about three rainy days, whereas in October you should expect about six.

In December and January you will need real rainwear. With about 18 rainy days per month, there's little chance of getting a decent tan.

Forest Fires

It is a sad fact of everyday life on the island that each and every summer there will be small, and larger, field and forest fires. However, several years ago almost one quarter of the forest area of Rhodes was destroyed by a huge fire that cut right across the island. Tragically, the cause of the fire has never been determined. Although even a splinter of glass lying in the right place can cause a fire if the sun

hits it at the correct angle, the most common causes of forest fires are carelessness and arson. The fire watch which was instituted after the great island fire is designed to spot and fight potential forest fires. The fire watch 'brigade' is spread over the entire island and members are in constant radio contact so that trucks and airplanes can be called in immediately to dowse the flames. Once a fire has occurred, however, the damage is usually irreparable. As a result, the erosion of the island's soil escalates, promoting catastrophic flooding, such as the village of Lardos has experienced since the great forest fire.

Greek environmental activists have contributed much, through private initiatives and voluntary labour, to the reforestation of a portion of the burned woodland.

When camping and walking, the vacationer is advised to exercise the greatest possible caution. Never *ever* throw cigarettes or matches from cars or buses.

GETTING AROUND

Ship Connections

Visitors may sign on for cruises around the island and to other islands in the Dodecanese. The cruise schedule may be obtained from the tourist office in the Nea Agora in Mandraki or from the following agencies:

1. Kamiros/Ialyssos/Rhodes: DANE, Odos Amerikis 95, Tel: 30930.
2. Paloma/Ag. Raphael: Red Sea, Odos Theodorakis 13, Tel: 27721.
3. Verginia/Papadiamantis: Kouros Travel, Odos Karpathou 34, Tel: 24377.
4. Daliana: Kydon Agency, Et. Dodekanissiou, Tel: 23000

There are also daily excursions to the islands of Kos and Symi. Check with Castelania Travel Service, Hippocrates Square, Old Quarter, Tel: 75860.

For further information: Rhodes Port Authority. Tel: 27690 or 22220.

If you are travelling by boat to surrounding countries such as Cyprus, Israel and Egypt, bear in mind that immigration authorities are especially strict with visitors arriving at their ports. Make sure you are carrying plenty of money and an onward ticket and preferably a credit card.

Turkey

If you fly to Rhodes on a direct charter flight via Athens, with no intermediate stop, you will not be permitted to visit Turkey, only a few hours journey by ship from Rhodes, for longer than 24 hours.

All other travellers—those who came to the island by ship or scheduled air carrier—are subject to no such restrictions.

Those who want to return to Rhodes from Turkey must prepare for rigorous customs checks.

Those who wish to travel in Turkey for longer that 24 hours must present their passports 24 hours ahead of departure time in the travel office.

Taxis

The central taxi stand in Rhodes City is located on the Plateia Rimini in Mandraki.

To order a taxi by phone: Tel: 27666. This number serves the entire island. Within the city limits of Rhodes City, you pay the basic fare. Double fares apply for all journeys outside the capital.

Bus Connections

The island of Rhodes has a well developed bus network which connects all villages with Rhodes City. The timetable varies seasonally. The central bus terminal in Rhodes City is located in the Nea Agora in Mandraki where bus schedules are posted. For information outside the capital, you can phone 20236. Within Rhodes City, call RODA: 27462.

Vehicle Rental

In Rhodes City you will find representatives of the big international auto rental firms such as Hertz, Avis and Inter-rent, whose prices are standardised and currently stand at about £35 ($70US) per day. Local Greek firms offer their vehicles at substantially cheaper rates, particularly off season, when competition is stiffest. If you waive a receipt and take the car for several weeks, you can get rates of around £25 ($50US) per day off season. The disadvantages of renting from Greek firms is that their vehicles are often in very poor condition, and you are usually barred from using them off paved roads.

In theory there are motorcycles for rent almost everywhere, but 500cc machines are available only in Rhodes City and Archangelos. For tours in the hinterland an Enduro (cross-country motorbike) is recommended. These rent for about £8.50 ($17US) per day.

Traffic Regulations

Although the locals appear to take little notice of many traffic rules, foreigners should follow them as best they can. (In the event of accident, tourists are not operating from a position of power, to put it diplomatically.)

Within village limits, the highest permissible speed is 50kph (30mph). On island roads (outside towns), 80kph (c.50mph) is the limit. The allowable blood alcohol level is 0.05 percent. Police checks are very seldom carried out, but that's no reason to throw caution to the wind.

Due to the fact that the armed forces travel on the roads at night—without lights—you must expect that behind every curve there may lurk an invisible, but solid, military convoy. Drive cautiously and be prepared for anything!

Fuel

In the rural south, service stations are further apart than in the developed north. All island petrol stations close daily at 7pm. Since the petrol available on Rhodes is rather low octane, you should always fill your car with premium. This is a standard requirement for rental cars. Lead free petrol is available only in Rhodes City.

The price of petrol corresponds roughly to prices charged elsewhere in Europe (around three times the price in the US). Diesel fuel, however, costs only about half the European price, since Greek vehicles using diesel fuel are used primarily in agriculture, which is subsidised in part through cheaper diesel prices.

HEALTH & EMERGENCIES

Pharmacies/Chemists

You will find chemists on virtually every street corner. Hours: Monday, Tuesday, Thursday and Friday, from 8am–1pm, and 5pm–9pm; Wednesday and Saturday, they close at 2pm. The address of the 24-hour pharmacy, open on a rotating basis, is listed in every pharmacy window.

Lindos, Archangelos and Lardos each have a pharmacy. In Lindos there is, in addition, an ambulance, which administers first aid in emergencies.

In **Gennadion**, there is a medical station located on the coast road as you enter the village. It also sells medications.

One further bit of information. In Greece, many medications are available without prescription. Among these are sulphanilamide and tranquillizers.

Hospitals

Hospital Vassilissas Olgas
General Red Cross Hospital
Rhodes City
Ambulance available around the clock.
Office hours: 7.30am–2.30pm.
Tel: 25555

First Aid

Ialyssos: Tel: 92285
Kalithea: Tel: 85209
Kremasti: Tel: 91222
Paradissi: Tel: 91355

Dentistry

Georgios Papazachariou
Iroon Polytechniou, 32, Rhodes
Tel: 24516

Dermatology (and Sexually Transmitted Diseases)

Michael S Savingos
Clinic: Venotocleon 1177, Tel: 28391
Practice: Tel: 34157

Eye, Ear, Nose and Throat

Alexander Noulis
D Themeli 83, Tel: 27835
Private: 22427

Pathology

Nikos Konsolos
Sofouli, Rhodes, Tel: 26316
Christos Efthimou
Agiou Anastasias 9, Rhodes, Tel: 29195

Gynaecology

Antony Perides
Clinic: G Efstathiou 11–13, Tel: 21601
Private: Canada 103, Tel: 23846

Bacteriology

Yannis A Minetos
Sof. Venizolou 1, Tel: 29864.
Private: Tel: 23424
Dimitra Mitroyanni
Ierou Lohou 11, Tel: 29744

Orthopaedics
Nicolaos Tiliakos
Ierou Lohou 14, Tel: 27818.
Private: Venotokleon 135

Ophthalmology
Sotirious Karahalios
Sof. Venizelou 1, Tel: 28954
Maria Tandidou
G Efstathiou 8, Tel: 23244

Pediatrics
Nikos K.Pavlides
D. Themeli 83, Tel: 28928
Antonis Papakonstantinou
Efstathiou 7, Tel: 2657. Private: 34031

Police
Police emergency in Rhodes City Tel: 104
Tourist Police Tel: 27423
Airport Police Tel: 92881
Ialyssos Tel: 92210
Afantou Tel: 51222
Harbour Police Tel: 27690/22220

Consulates
Austria	Tel: 22393
Belgium	Tel: 24661
Denmark	Tel: 30569
Germany	Tel: 30569
Finland	Tel: 20120
France	Tel: 27413
Great Britain	Tel: 27247
Italy	Tel: 27432
Norway	Tel: 24061
Spain	Tel: 22460
Sweden	Tel: 31822
Turkey	Tel: 23362

POST & COMMUNICATION

Post
Main Post Office, Rhodes City.
Mandraki, Odos Eleftherias, Tel: 22212. Hours: Monday–Friday, 7am–8.30pm.

In addition, postage stamps are available at kiosks and stationers/newsagents throughout the island.

Telephone
Although you can make telephone calls at most post offices (*takithromeíon*), the organization called OTE (o-táy) is responsible for telephone and telegraph services, and maintains offices in all of the larger towns. A semi-public telephone is obligatory in the smaller villages, usually to be found in a *kafeneíon* or store. Here you can telephone at the standard rates. All other telephones, in bars, restaurants, hotels, etc can charge whatever they wish for calls, and do.

Dialling internationally is reasonably straightforward. The international access code from Greece is 00. After this, dial the relevant country code: Australia (61); Canada (1); Germany (49); Italy (39); Japan (81); the Netherlands (31); Spain (34); United Kingdom (44); United States (1). If you're using a US phone credit card, dial the company's access number listed below—AT&T, Tel: 00-800-1311; MCI, Tel: 00-800-1211.

Area Codes
Athens	01
Thessaloniki	031
Kos, Nissiros, Astipalea	0242
Kalimnos	0243
Karpathos, Kassos	0245
Leros, Lipsi, Patmos	0247

Local Codes
The island of Rhodes is divided into three networks: the northern sector of the island, up to Soroni on the west coast and Afantou on the east coast, has the area code 0241, which is also used for the islands of Chalki, Kastellorizo, Symi and Tilos. The southwest sector of the island, and the towns of Embonas, Salakos, Monolithos and Apolakkia, has the area code 0246. The southeast sector, and the villages of Archangelos, Lindos, Lardos, Gennadion and Kataria has the area code 0244.

Radio

Radio ERT 2 broadcasts English language news at 2.25pm daily.

FESTIVALS & HOLIDAYS

National Holidays

25 March, Independence Day. On this day in 1821 the revolt against Turkish rule began. The day is celebrated with military and school parades.

28 September, Ohi Day. On this day in 1940 the Greek government defied Mussolini's ultimatum demanding capitulation without resistance. Because of this historic 'no', the day is called Ohi Day.

Religious Festivals

Greek Orthodox Easter is the most important festival of the year. The high point is Easter Mass, which is celebrated at midnight on Easter Saturday/Sunday. Afterwards, the fasting period ends and people gather for a feast.

23 April, Aghios Georgios, celebrated at Kritinia.

Beginning of June, great monastery festival at Moni Thari.

24 June, Summer Solstice, marked by many island celebrations.

29 June, Sts Petros and Pavlos, special festivities at St Paul's Bay at Lindos.

17 July, Aghia Marina, at Paradissi.

20 July, Profitis Ilias, in front of Ilias Church on Mt Profitis Ilias.

27 July 27, Aghios Panteleimonas, at Siana.

29/30 July, Aghios Soulas at St Silas at Soroni with competitive events and donkey races.

6 August, Metamorfosis, at Maritsa.

14-23 August, Panageia Festival at Kremasti.

15 August, Dormition of the Virgin, celebrated throughout the island and the rest of Greece.

8 September, Festival of the Holy Virgin at Moni Tsambica, Moni Skiadi and Embonas.

18 September, Aghios Loukas at Afantou.

Holiday Surcharges

From Christmas until 6 January, as well as during the Orthodox Easter season, *tavérnes*, restaurants, and taxi drivers demand a surcharge. The taxi 'gift' (*thóro*) runs about 35p (70¢US); in restaurants, you are charged roughly 10 percent extra.

PHOTOGRAPHY

In the larger villages colour negative as well as slide film is available. The prices are, however, between one third and 50 percent higher than in northern Europe and America. It is therefore a good idea to bring a supply of film along with you, protected in a lead pouch available at photographic supply stores.

ETIQUETTE

Salutations

In Greek cities, as elsewhere in the 'developed' West, people pass on the street without greeting one another. However, in Rhodes' villages, it is actually *de rigeur* for visitors to greet

the locals if they want to avoid offending.

From dawn till about 3pm, one says *Kaliméra* (good day). *(Kaliméra sas* is the polite/plural form.) Until nightfall, upon arriving, and until about 8pm upon departing, you say *Kalispéra (Kalispéra sas)*. On the other hand, you say *Kaliníkta* upon arriving after midnight and on departure after 8pm. If this gets too complicated for you, simply say *Yássou* (familiar/singular form) or *Yássas* (polite/plural form). See the section *The Greek Language* on page 95 for a lengthier introduction to Demotic Greek. Master the rudiments, and Rhodian friends will be both surprised and pleased.

Nudism

There are no official nudist beaches on Rhodes. Nevertheless, over time, topless bathing has prevailed on all the larger beaches, and you need no longer fear being arrested for wearing only half your bikini. On beaches in

Golf

There is an eight-hole golf course at Afantou. Information may be obtained by calling 51451 or 51255/6/7.

Sailing

Information is available at the Rhodes Yacht Club, Rhodes City, Plateia Kountouriou 9, Tel: 23287; or, Camper and Nicholson's Yacht Agency, 26 Amerikis Street, Tel: 22927/30504/-30505.

Tennis

Tennis Club Rhodos, Konstantinou 20, Tel: 25705.

In addition, most of the large hotels in Rhodes City have tennis courts which are accessible to the general public.

Underwater Sports

From 1 May through October, the Rhodos Subaqua Centre offers diving

the south, which are usually semi deserted, you can skinny dip with confidence, as long as there are no Greek families in the vicinity who might be easily offended.

You should not visit beach restaurants in bathing costumes, let alone in an even greater state of undress. (Believe it or not, this has been known to happen.)

courses with professional instruction. You can learn about other services of the club (including boat piloting) by calling 33654.

Courses are also offered by the official School for Underwater Sport, Koulia, Tel: 22296.

Important: If you dive on your own, you should know that diving for archaeological artefacts in the waters off Rhodes is *strictly* forbidden.

Windsurfing

All of the larger hotels on the island maintain equipment for wind surfers. The west coast at Ixia and Vliha Bay near Lindos are ideal for this sport. Only for the experienced is Cape Prassonissi, on the southern tip of the island. You can get further information at the Tourist Offices in Rhodes City or Lindos.

Riding

Mike's Horses, Tel: 21387, open 9am–1pm, and 4pm–8m. The stables are on the road to Ialyssos/Filerimos.

Hunting

Information is provided at the Hunters' Association in the Nea Agora; Tel: 21481.

CULTURE

Theatre

In summer (April to October), a Sound and Light show takes place every evening near the Nea Agora. The show is presented in English, German, Swedish and French. Information about starting times is available at the entrance.

In the Old Quarter, Greek Folk Dances are presented daily, except Saturday, at 9.15pm in Plateia Poli during summer. Further information: Tel: 20157 or 20085.

The current program of the Rhodian National Theatre is available at the Tourist Information office.

Cinemas

Rhodes City has several cinemas, the addresses and programs of which are available at the Tourist Office.

Lindos also has a cinema, which is open only in summer.

Museums

In general, the museums on Rhodes are open daily, except Monday, from 8.30am–3pm. Admission is free on Sunday.

Since the crush of visitors is heavy, you must expect doors to be shut in your face at 2pm. This applies particularly to the Acropolis of Lindos.

RELIGION

Places of Worship

Roman Catholic Churches: Both Santa Maria and San Francisco are open continuously.
Mosques: On Friday evening Moslems meet for prayer in the Suleiman Pasha Mosque on Odos Sokratous.
Jewish Synagogue: The Synagogue Shalom, near Plateia Evreon, is open continuously.

USEFUL INFORMATION

Snakes

There *are* snakes on Rhodes, but the majority of these are non-poisonous. Vipers are the only snakes whose bite can be dangerous, but snake bite can be treated immediately at any medical station. Viper bites are unusual on the island since the snakes hurriedly slip away at the slightest vibration of approaching feet. In May and June you may also encounter snakes in the villages, since they like to lay their eggs where there is masonry. This is no reason to nurture exaggerated fears, as snakes are deathly afraid of people.

Toilets

On occasion, the hygienic standard of Rhodian plumbing leaves much to be desired, although the traditional, Turkish-style squat-toilet has been replaced almost everywhere by Western fixtures. (There's a lot to be said—by physicians—for the former system, but this is not the place to elaborate.) Since there is no mains drainage on Rhodes, toilet paper (and all other paper waste) should be thrown into the bucket standing by the toilet. Sometimes, tourists complain that these pails have no lids or are overflowing, but if you consider the difficulty of waste disposal and the numbers of visitors who descend on the island in summer, perhaps you will be a little more understanding.

The Greek Language

Greek is a phonetic language. There are some combinations of vowels and consonants which customarily stand for certain sounds, and some slight pronunciation changes determined by what letter follows but, generally, sounds are pronounced as they are written, without additions or omissions. Thus, learning the phonetic values of the Greek alphabet, and then reading, say, street sounds out loud, is a good method of getting the feel of the language. Most Rhodians have some knowledge of English, and most Greeks are delighted to find a visitor making stabs at speaking Greek. (Unlike Parisians, the Greeks do not ridicule you for making mistakes: they themselves have a hard time with Greek spelling

and the complicated Greek grammar.) Whatever you can accomplish, guide book in hand, will be rewarded.

In addition to pronouncing each letter, you should remember that stress plays an important role in Modern Greek. When you learn a Greek word, learn where the stress falls at the same time. Each Greek word has a single stress (marked in the following vocab-

ulary list with an accent). Greek is an inflected language as well, and noun and adjective endings change according to gender, number and case. Case endings, the rules governing them, and the conjugation of Greek verbs, are beyond the scope of a guide. (For visitors staying on for longer, there are language classes at the Hellenic American Union and other teaching centres in Athens. In the islands, Greek friends may trade Greek lessons for English, hour for hour. This not only improves your Greek; it cements friendships.)

The Greek Alphabet

CAP.	L.C.	VALUE	NAME
A	α	a in father	alfa
B	β	v in visa	vita
Γ	γ	ghama	
		gh before consonants and a, o and oo; y before e, as in year	
Δ	δ	th in then	thelta
E	ε	e in let	epsilon
Z	ζ	z in zebra	zita
H	η	e in keep	ita
Θ	θ	th in theory	thita
I	ι	e in keep	yota
K	κ	k in king	kapa
Λ	l	l in million	lamda
M	μ	m in mouse	mi
N	ν	n in no	ni
Ξ	ξ	ks in jacks	ksi
O	o	o in oh	omikron
Π	π	p in pebble	pi
P	ρ	r in raisin	ro
Σ	σ	s in sun	sigma
T	τ	t in trireme	taf
E	ε	e in keep	ipsilon
Φ	φ	f in favor	fi
X	χ	h in help	hi
Ψ	ψ	ps in copse	psi
Ω	ω	o in oh	omega

Dipthongs

Type	Value
αι	e in let
αυ	av or af in avert or after
ει	e in keep
ευ	ev or ef
οι	e in keep
ου	oo in poor

Double consonants

μπ	b at beginnings of words; mb in the middle of words
ντ	d at beginnings of words; nd in the middle of words
τζ	dz as in adze
γγ, γκ	gh at the beginnings of words; ng in the middle of words

Vocabulary

Pronounce e as in pet; a as in father; i as in keep; o as in oh.

Numbers

one	é-na (neuter)/ é-nas(masc.)/mí-a(fem.)
two	thí-o
three	trí-a(neuter)/tris (masc. and fem.)
four	té-se-ra
five	pén-de
six	ék-si
seven	ep-tá
eight	ok-tó
nine	e-né-a
ten	thé-ka
eleven	én-the-ka
twelve	thó-the-ka
thirteen	the-ka-trí-a/the-ka-trís
fourteen	the-ka-té-se-ra
etc. until twenty.	
twenty	í-ko-si
twenty-one	í-ko-si é-na (neuter and masc.)/ í-ko-si mí-a (fem.)
thirty	tri-án-da
forty	sa-rán-da
fifty	pe-nín-da
sixty	ek-sín-da
seventy	ev-tho-mín-da
eighty	og-thón-da
ninety	e-ne-nín-da
one hundred	e-ka-tó
one hundred and fifty	e-ka-to-pe-nín-da
two hundred	thi-a-kó-si-a (neuter)
three hundred	tri-a-kó-si-a (neuter)
four hundred	te-tra-kó-si-a (neuter)
one thousand	hí-lia (neuter)

Days of the Week

Monday	Thef-té-ra
Tuesday	Trí-ti
Wednesday	Te-tár-ti
Thursday	Pém-pti
Friday	Pa-ras-ke-ví
Saturday	Sá-va-to
Sunday	Ki-ri-a-kí
yesterday	kthes

today	sí-me-ra	ticket	i-si-tí-ri-o
tomorrow	á-vri-o	road/street	thró-mos/o-thós
		beach	pa-ra-lí-a
Greetings		sea	thá-la-sa
Hello	yá sas (plural/polite)	church	e-kli-sí-a
	yá sou (sing./familiar)	ancient ruin	ar-hé-a
	ya (abbreviated)	centre	kén-tro
Good day	ká-li mé-ra	square	pla-tí-a
Good evening	ka-li spe-ra		
Good night	káli ník-ta	**Hotels**	
How are you?	Ti ká-ne-te?	hotel	kse-no-tho-hí-o
	(plural/polite)	**Do you have a room?**	
	Ti ká-nis? (singular/		É-hie-te é-na tho-má-
	familiar)		ti-o?
fine (in response)		bed	kre-vá-ti
	ka-lá	**shower with hot water**	
pleased to meet you			douz me zes-tó ne-ró
	há-ri-ka	key	kli-thí
		entrance	í-so-thos
Getting Around		exit	ék-so-thos
yes	ne	toilet	toua-lé-ta
no	ó-hi	women's	yi-ne-kón
okay	en dák-si	men's	án-dron
thank you	ef-ha-ris-tó		
very much	pá-ra po-lí	**Shopping**	
excuse me	sig-nó-mi	store	ma-ga-zí
it doesn't matter		kiosk	pe-ríp-te-ro
	then bi-rá-zi	open/shut	a-nik-tó/klis-tó
it's nothing	tí-po-ta	post office	ta-ki-thro-mí-o
certainly/polite yes		stamp	gra-ma-tó-simo
	má-li-sta	letter	grá-ma
Can I..?	Bó-ro na..?	envelope	fá-ke-lo
When?	Pó-te?	telephone	ti-lé-fo-no
Where is..?	Pou í-n-e..?	bank	trá-pe-za
Do you speak English		marketplace	a-go-rá
	mi-lá-te ta an-gli-ka	Have you..?	É-hie-te..?
What time is it?		Is there..?	É-hi..?
	Ti ó-ra i-ne?	**How much does it cost?**	
What time will it leave?			Pó-so ká-ni?
	Ti ó-ra tha fi-gi	**It's (too) expensive**	
I want	thé-lo		I-ne (po-lí) a-kri-vó
here/there	e-thó/e-kí	How much?	Pó-so?
near/far	kon-dá/ma-kri-á	How many?	Pó-sa?
small/large	mi-kró/me-gá-lo		
good/bad	ka-ló/ka-kó	**Emergencies**	
warm/cold	zes-tó/krí-o	doctor	ya-trós
bus	le-o-for-í-on	hospital	no-so-ko-mí-o
boat	ka-rá-vi, va-pó-ri	pharmacy	far-ma-kí-o
bike/moped	po-thí-la-to/	police	as-ti-no-mí-a
	mo-to-po-thí-la-to	station	stath-mós

97

ART/PHOTO CREDITS

Cover Design	Klaus Geisler
Cartography	Berndtson & Berndtson
Photography by	Presto Press *and*
20	Rob Cheeves
10/11	Plerre Couteau
23, 28, 35	John Decopoulos
5, 44, 71	Chris Jones
27, 34, 57 top, 59	D and I Mathioulakis
14	National Archaeological Museum
18	V Sekellarides
19	M Stournara
15, 16,	M Toubis
21	E Tzaferis
6/7	Bill Wassman

ENGLISH EDITION

Edited and Revised by	Elizabeth Boleman-Herring
Production Editor	Gareth Walters
Managing Editor	Andrew Eames

INSIGHT GUIDES

COLORSET NUMBERS

You'll find the colorset number on the spine of each Insight Guide.

INSIGHT *Pocket* GUIDES

• •

United States: **Houghton Mifflin Company, Boston MA 02108**
Tel: (800) 2253362 Fax: (800) 4589501

Canada: **Thomas Allen & Son, 390 Steelcase Road East**
Markham, Ontario L3R 1G2
Tel: (416) 4759126 Fax: (416) 4756747

Great Britain: **GeoCenter UK, Hampshire RG22 4BJ**
Tel: (256) 817987 Fax: (256) 817988

Worldwide: **Höfer Communications Singapore 2262**
Tel: (65) 8612755 Fax: (65) 8616438

" I was first drawn to the Insight Guides by the excellent "Nepal" volume. I can think of no book which so effectively captures the essence of a country. Out of these pages leaped the Nepal I know – the captivating charm of a people and their culture. I've since discovered and enjoyed the entire Insight Guide Series. Each volume deals with a country or city in the same sensitive depth, which is nowhere more evident than in the superb photography. "

Sir Edmund Hillary